THE CHUMPI STONE GUIDEBOOK:
Carved Companions from the Andes

Written and Illustrated by Drake Bear Stephen

Wisdom Weaver Press

THE CHUMPI STONE GUIDEBOOK:
Carved Companions from the Andes

Written and Illustrated by: Drake Bear Stephen

Copyright © 2021 Drake Bear Stephen
Except as acknowledged. All rights reserved.

No part of this book may be reproduced in whole or in part, stored in a retrieval system, or transmitted in any form or by any means electronic, mechanical, photocopying, recording, or otherwise, without written permission from the copyright holder, except brief quotations used in a review.

Although the authors and publisher have made every effort to ensure the accuracy and completeness of information contained in this book, we assume no responsibility for errors, inaccuracies, omissions, or any inconsistency herein. Any slights of people, places, or organizations are unintentional.

Published by: Wisdom Weaver Press
PO Box 888
Clayton, CA 94517
ISBN #: 978-0-9862498-5-3
Library of Congress PCN#: TBD
Library of Congress Title: The chumpi stone guidebook

Printed in the United States of America.
First printing, March 2021

TABLE OF CONTENTS

1 INTRODUCTION	**1**
Definition of Chumpi Stones	2
Background Information	3
Uses for Chumpi Stones	4
2 CHUMPI STONES 101	**7**
Anatomy of a Chumpi Stone	8
Obtaining Chumpi Stones	8
Carving Styles	10
Unique Chumpi Stones	10
Material Correspondences	12
Color Correspondences	18
Number Correspondences	22
Textile Correspondences	25
3 CHUMPI STONE CORRESPONDENCES	**33**
Cosmology by the Numbers (0 through 12)	34
Summary of Chumpi Stone Correspondences	61
4 OTHER CARVED COMPANIONS	**63**
Taway (Dice)	64
Tiha Rumi (Tile Stones)	65
Makikuna (Hands)	66
Conopakuna (Votive Offerings)	67

5 VISUAL DIRECTORY OF CARVED IMAGES — 69

- Images are Mythic Stories — 70
- Directory of Images — 72

6 CHUMPI STONE USES — 77

- A Birthing Ritual for Chumpi Stones — 78
- Cleansing Chumpi Stones — 78
- Energizing Chumpi Stones — 80
- Affirmation Work — 81
- Divination Work — 85

7 ENERGY WORK WITH CHUMPI STONES — 87

- The Energy Body — 88
- The Andean Energy System — 90
- The Hindu Energy System — 93
- Energy Transmission Work — 96
- Healing with Chumpi Stones — 102
- Grids for Healing Work — 103

6 APPENDIXES: ILLUSTRATIONS — 107

- Chumpi Stone Worksheet — 108
- Map of Sacred Valley — 109
- Inka Tawantinsuyu — 110
- Chakanasuyu Cosmology — 111
- HANAN and hurin — 112
- Medicine Wheel of Andean Cosmology — 113
- Fun with Chumpikuna — 114

7 GLOSSARY — 117

8 REFERENCE LINKS — 131

9 WISDOM WEAVER PRESS OFFERINGS — 133

10 ACKNOWLEDGEMENTS — 135

11 ABOUT THE AUTHOR — 137

> "Many people cannot refrain from picking up stones of a slightly unusual color or shape and keeping them, without knowing why they do this. It is as if the stones hold a living mystery that fascinates them. [Humans] have collected stones since the beginning of time and have apparently assumed that certain ones were the containers of the life-force with all of its mystery."
>
> –Carl Jung

CHAPTER 1

INTRODUCTION

DEFINITION OF CHUMPI STONES

Chumpi (also spelled *chunpi*) is a Quechua word that has two literal meanings: "brown" and "belt". Both of these meanings can be applied to the fascinating stones that are carved with humps on them. *Chumpi rumi* are also called "*apu* stones" because the humps carved in them represent mountains. They have also been called a "*mullu khuya*" because it is believed the original stones were carved from a spondylus (spiny oyster) shell, called "*mullu*" in Quechua. Today a majority of the stones are carved from *huamanga* (alabaster), which is then dyed a brown color. The original use for the stones was to weave together the energetic belts surrounding the physical body.

English speakers usually refer to a *chumpi* stone as "stone" however, technically they are *chumpi rumi* or *chumpi khuya*. The Quechua term for stone is "*rumi*" and the plural form is "*rumikuna*". When a *rumi* is used for sacred purposes it is called "*khuya*" (*khuyakuna* is the plural form), which comes from the Quechua word "*qhuyay*," meaning to love or deeply care for. *Rumi* are conscious living beings sourced from Mother Earth so they hold her permanence, stability, reliability, and immortality. As pieces of Mother Earth, they can collect, hold, and transmute energy that can be used for focusing intention, grounding, and healing.

> "The word '*khuya*' literally means affection. The five *chumpi khuyakuna* are infused with your *sami* (high vibratory energy), personal power, and *munay* (love). In this way, they are holy stones."
>
> –Joan Parisi Wilcox, author of *Masters of the Living Energy: The Mystical World of the Q'ero of Peru*

Chumpi stones originated in the Andean region of Peru but today, they have migrated into mainstream cultures around the world. In this way, ancient practices are being adapted for our modern culture. This guidebook will expand on the meanings and uses for *chumpi* stones.

> "Each *chumpi* [stone] corresponds to a specific *apu* (mountain). Both the stone you hold in your hand and the great mountain in the Andes are physical and energetic embodiments of one of the fundamental facets of universal consciousness, circling from Birth all the way through to Creation. To hold symbols of the *apukuna* in your hands is to tap into this great flow of cosmic information."
>
> –Eleanora Amendolara, author of *Chumpi Illumination: Gateways to Healing and Transformation*

Chumpi stones are energetic companions that can activate, animate, and move energy within different grids of time, dimensions, and portals. In this way, they are a synergy of energy exchanges. *Chumpi* stones are living beings. They will talk to you if you listen carefully. They can:

1. Carry and connect energy.
2. Direct or guide energy through their points.
3. Project a geometric energy body into space.
4. Open energetic portals to your inner and outer space.
5. Bridge the *apukuna* (mountain spirits) to the *chaskakuna* (stars) and *Pachamama* (Mother Earth) to the *Hanaqpacha* (Cosmos, celestial heavens).
6. Access the *Hanaqpacha* and anchor cosmic energy in the *Kaypacha* (our physical world).
7. Bridge us to the physical objects in the universe.
8. Bridge us to our *chakras*, that anchor the energy body to the physical body.

So, while perusing this guidebook, you will find yourself strolling along *Apu* Avenue amongst the mystery and majesty of *chumpi* stones, who will provide you with magic of companionship.

> "*Chumpi* stones are ancient tools of the *paq'o* (the medicine men and women of the high mountains of Peru). *Chumpi* stone sets are intimately connected to the wisdom and power of the *Apus* (the mountain spirits). As such, they are seen as empowered stones, and have direct relationship to the stars. Used for initiation, healing, and transformation, *Chumpi* stone sets are the voice of the Andean Cosmology and shamans' way. These sets, hand-crafted in the Sacred Valley of Peru (a map is shown in the Appendix), are intentionally small in order to fit nicely in our hands, easily enhance the work of the *mesa* (sacred medicine bundle), and are portals to the divine."
>
> —Robert Wakeley Wheeler, co-author of *The Chakana Oracle: Ancient Wisdom for the 21st Century*

BACKGROUND INFORMATION

Chumpi stones are sacred tools used by the Q'ero and other indigenous people of the Andes. The Q'ero belong to the largest Quechua-speaking group in the high Andes of South America. They are potato farmers, alpaca and llama herders, musicians, and weavers that live in remote villages at 14,000 to 18,000 feet (4,267 to 5,486 meters).

The Qer'o were the spiritual advisors to the Inka. Since the Spanish conquistador invasion, they have preserved their indigenous ethnic identity, becoming the guardians of the wisdom of the Andes. They are earth-focused, making offerings to *Pachamama* (Mother Earth) and the *Apukuna* (mountain spirits), for the well-being of themselves, their animals, and their crops.

The major philosophical tenets of their simple way of life are based on *ayni*, the principle of reciprocity, and animism, the belief in the animated essence of all things.

The Q'ero and other indigenous people of the Andes are known for the beauty of their traditional textiles and the power of their carved items. Images on both the textiles and their carvings represent messages received from their ancestors and the invisible energetic universe.

> "The term Cosmovision refers to a way of understanding and relating to reality. The Andean Cosmovision is not intellectual in nature. It is not a set of ideas or beliefs. It simply cannot be defined, described, or encompassed with word or thought. It can, however, be experienced and it can be explored. Eventually you come to understand the Cosmovision, but this understanding is not intellectual, it is an understanding that develops at a deeper level of your Being."
>
> –Oakley E. Gordon, author of *The Andean Cosmovision*

You can experience the *chumpi* stones in the indigenous way by holding each, one at a time, while you sit in quiet meditation and listen for messages or wait for visions that will give you impressions of how to work with your stones.

It is the Western way to document experience in language. Therefore, I offer this guidebook on *chumpi* stone correspondences. Since I am not physically descended from the Inka or Q'ero, my cultural knowledge is not complete. However, I hope I have honored their ancestral lineage with this guidebook. I encourage you to experience the *chumpi* stones in the way that resonates with you. I present this material in the spirit of cultural appreciation.

USES FOR CHUMPI STONES

As mentioned above, the original intent of the *chumpi* stones was probably to weave the energetic belts or bands surrounding the physical body. (This process is described beginning on page 96.) There may have been other uses for these stones that have been lost over time. Since there were no written languages during the Inka Empire, all of the traditions were handed down orally from generation to generation.

It is believed that *chumpi* stones were also buried in the earth as a form of gratitude to *Pachamama* (Mother Earth) or as a petition for healthy crops. And there is evidence that *chumpi* stones that were carved from *hiwaya* (meteorite stone) were used as weapons.

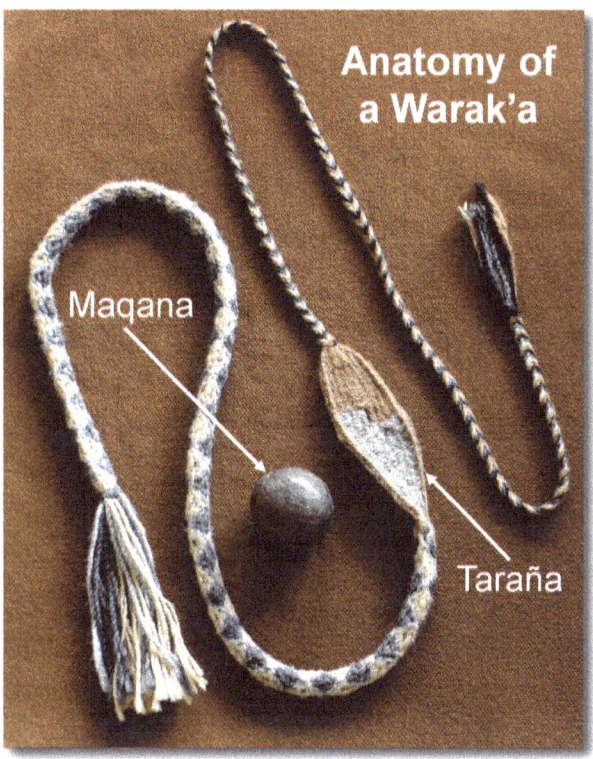

A *warak'a* or *huaraca* (*boleadora* in Spanish) is a braided rope typically made from natural alpaca or llama fiber. It normally has a looped end that attaches to the hand and a center *taraña* (saddle) for the positioning of a stone. The stone is called a *maqana* or *macana rumi* (fighting stone) usually carved from *hiwaya*. The stone gets hurled from the *warak'a* like a slingshot. The *warak'a* is also used when herding llama.

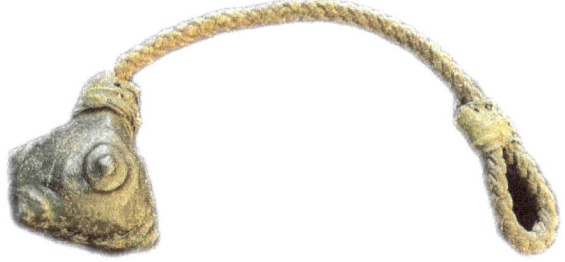

Sometimes a *chumpi* stone was used as *maqana*. The weapon in the photo above is of a *chumpi* stone attached to a *waska* (woven rope). In this case, it would have been used by twirling it to hit a target. Was the *chumpi* stone used because it is made of heavy meteorite material or because it has a special sacred meaning? I would guess it was used for both reasons because one of the fundamental concepts in the cosmology of the indigenous people of the Andes is the principle of duality. Therefore, every object has a physical presence with a literal purpose as well as an energetic presence with a spiritual meaning.

Lately, additional uses for *chumpi* stones have been identified. They include:

1. **MOVING ENERGY** – *Chumpi* stones have the capability to attract, propel, repel, radiate, and transform energy in ritual and ceremony.

2. **HOLDING ENERGETIC SPACE** – *Chumpi* stones can be used to create sacred boundaries in rituals and ceremonies. A *huaca* is a sacred place where energy is held. *Chumpi* stones can be used to define a place or portal of power.

3. **OPENING PORTALS TO OTHER DIMENSIONS** – *Chumpi* stones open portals to explore other dimensions that offer an infinite number of possibilities.

4. **MEDITATING AND JOURNEYING COMPANIONS** – Hold a stone while journeying or meditating to support or augment the theme of your meditation or journey. (See correspondences in chapters 2 and 3)

5. **PERFORMING KARPAYS** – *Chumpi* stones transmit energy in sacred ceremonies. The two rites that use *chumpi* stones are "*Chumpi Away* (Belt Weaving)" and the "*Ayni Karpay* (Right Relationship Transmission)". (See page 96)

6. **HEALING WORK** – Use *chumpi* stones to open up energy fields, *chakras*, and connecting to the universe in energy medicine sessions. (See page 102)

7. **MASSAGING** – Similar to using a crystal wand in massage, use *chumpi* points to release energy at trigger points and move energy through the physical and energetic body.

8. **CONNECTING ENERGETIC CORDS** – Use *chumpi* stones to connect to your *apukuna* (mountain spirits) and create energetic cords between them and you.

9. **MANIFESTING AND PROTECTION WORK** – Build and energize *chumpi* stone grids for manifesting and protection. (See page 81)

10. **DIVINING AN ANSWER** – Use a #1 *chumpi* stone to spin on a grid for divination purposes. (See page 85)

11. **CARRYING A DAILY COMPANION** – Choose a *chumpi* stone that will support your intention for the day and carry it with you all day.

12. **BURYING IN THE EARTH** – Bury *chumpi* stones on your property as an offering for *Pachamama* or as a petition for blessing and protection.

You may also create new purposes for your *chumpi* stones. Welcome them. The ancestors want *chumpi* stones to be a part of the 21st century.

CHAPTER 2

CHUMPI STONES 101

ANATOMY OF THE CHUMPI STONE

A *chumpi* stone usually has one to thirteen points carved into them. Each point is a representation of an *apu* (mountain). The mountains are powerful because they are the connection point to the stars. A point typically has three rings, but sometimes more, carved around it. These rings represent the three shamanic worlds: the *Hanaqpacha* (Upper World), the *Kaypacha* (Middle World), and the *Ukhupacha* (Lower World).

OBTAINING CHUMPI STONES

Chumpi stones are usually available in sets of five (representing the five energy bands of the body), seven (representing the colors of rainbow), nine (representing all of the single digit numbers), and twelve (representing the twelve points of the *chakana*, the Southern Cross star constellation).

Chumpi stones can also be purchased as individual stones. The very best place to obtain *chumpi* stones is in the Sacred Valley surrounding Cusco, Peru. Pisac is a gold mine for individuals that want to shop for antique stones. Most stones in the Pisac marketplace are sold individually, so the buyer can create their own unique set. However, if you aren't able to travel to the Andes, there is a list of online resources at the back of this guidebook. (See pages 131-132.)

Another alternative is to find a *chumpi* stone carver in Cusco, Peru and have a set created to your very own specifications. Robert Wakeley Wheeler has been working with carvers for years, purchasing *chumpi* stone sets in bulk and selling them on his website (www.sacredpathways.us/marketplace). Here you can find sets created from different materials other than the traditional *huamanga* (alabaster) and *hiwaya* (meteorite stone). One of the most powerful sets is made up of the seven colors of the rainbow all carved from crystals found in Peru. (For more details on these sets, please read further on in the Materials Correspondence section beginning on page 12.)

You may want to obtain more than one set. These stones have different properties depending on their color, size, material, and number of points. You can designate special purposes for some of your sets, for instance, using one set exclusively for yourself and using another set for working with others. I currently own more than a dozen sets and I am always open to finding new and unique sets to add to my collection.

A *chumpi* stone carver at work in Cusco.
Some carvers work solely with hand tools
while others also work with motorized tools.

CARVING STYLES

Carved images typically appear on *chumpi* stones made of *huamanga* (alabaster). Other items made of *huamanga* may also have carved images on them. These items include *taway* (dice), *tiha* (tiles), *maki* (hands), and *canopa* (votive vessels). These items and their images express the Inka energy tradition and the artistry of the Andean people.

There are two styles of carvings:

1. **HIGH RELIEF** (called "*altorrelieve*" in Spanish), where the image seems to be coming out of the stone towards us.

2. **LOW RELIEF** (called "*bajorrelieve*" in Spanish) or "etched" in English, where it seems we must go to the image.

UNIQUE CHUMPI STONES

The 7-Point Archetype

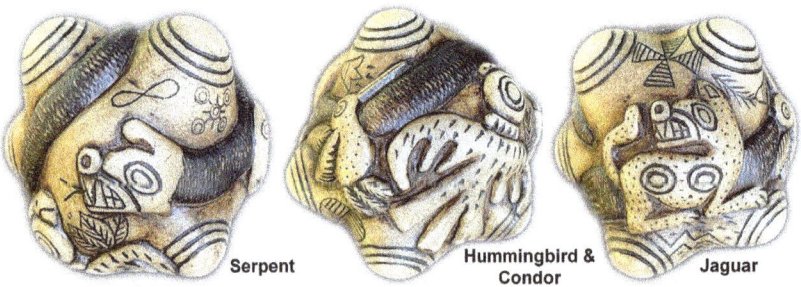

The Shaman's Market (www.ShamansMarket.com) sells incredibly beautiful and unique *chumpi* stones from Peruvian artists Abelardo and Luzmarina Mirano. The Shaman's Store website says, "[this couple's] art is infused with a deep understanding of Andean cosmology, ancient shamanic practices and a deep love for the *apukuna* (mountain spirits) and *Pachamama* (Mother Earth)". Their work is truly beautiful as well as powerful. The piece shown above has seven points that feature four Andean archetypes and other sacred symbols.

The following three stones were also created by Abelardo and Luzmarina Mirano (the 7-Point, 12-Point, and 13-Point).

The 7-Point Ñust'a

The seven points on this stone represent the seven *Ñust'a* (Female Nature Spirits or Goddesses of the Andes): Mama Ocllo, Doña Mujia, Mama Simona, Doña Theresa, Maria Sakapana, Doña Juana (Huana) Waman Tiklla, and Doña Tomasa Waman Tiklla.

The 12-Point Apu

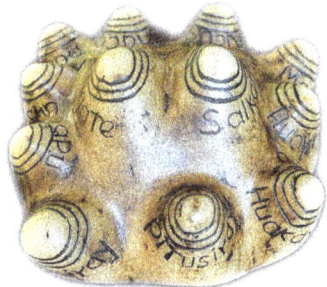

The twelve points on this stone represent twelve mountains in the sacred valley around Cusco. They are: Ausangate, Huacawilka (also called Huakaywillka, Veronica, Huacrahuilki "horn pass", Huacay Huilcay, Wayna Willka, Waqaywillka, and Urubamba), Huanacauri, Huayna Picchu, Machu Picchu, Mamasimon, Pachatusan, Pikol, Pitusiray, Putucus, Salcantay, and Sawasiray (Sahuasiyiray).

The 13-Point Killa

The thirteen points on this stone represent the thirteen moons of the year and honors the Inkan goddess, *Mama Killa* (Mother Moon).

MATERIALS CORRESPONDENCES

Chumpi stones are now being carved from many different types of stones and crystals. Because materials attract and hold light and vibration in different ways it is important to choose the material that will best complement the intention of the work you will use them for. Below is a list of these materials and their correspondences.

Spondylus (aka Mullu)

Lore says that the original *chumpi* stones were carved from the spondylus (spiny oyster) shell called *"mullu"*. This shell, found on the Peruvian coast, was used as far back as 4200 BCE to make jewelry and sacred items. Because this oyster was so rare, its flesh was considered to be a food of the Gods. Robert Wakeley Wheeler and I searched the markets in Cusco and Pisac to find a spondylus *chumpi* set with no success. However, we did find a dealer who sold us a spondylus shell from which we had several *chumpi* stone sets carved.

Huamanga (aka Alabaster or Calcite)

The most common material that *chumpi* stones are carved from is *huamanga*, which is a soft limestone, also known as alabaster. *Huamanga* originates from a city of the same name in Ayacucho, Peru. Once the stones are carved, they are coated with a brown ink-like paint. The Quechua name for brown is *"chumpi"*.

Alabaster aids memory and astral projection; balances yin/yang qualities and mental/emotional qualities.

Hiwaya (aka Meteorite Stone or Hematite Ore)

Carved Hiwaya Set   Uncarved Hiwaya Set

The second most common material used in *chumpi* sets is *hiwaya* (meteorite stone), which is a red or black hematite ore. These stones are found in the Andes mountains. Because of their origin and their magnetic characteristics, they are very powerful stones. *Hiwaya* stones usually do not have images carved on them.

Hiwaya is a good energy absorber, transmitter, and transducer. It aids in connection with spiritual and celestial beings and as well as exploration of past lives on other planets. The magnetic properties help align energy flows and create fields of attraction energy.

Amethyst Violet, Lavender, or Purple

Amethyst aids inner peace, calm, balance, intuition, insight, higher knowledge, wisdom, meditation, past life regression work, and psychic abilities. It is known as the Sobriety Stone and aids in addiction clearing.

Celestite (aka Celestine) Light Blue

Celestite aids meditation, astral travel, hope, celestial connection, and emotional protection. Balances thought processes and communication. It reduces worry, fear, and anxiety.

Chrysocolla (aka Peruvian Turquoise) Green or Aqua

Turquoise Chrysocolla aids creativity, communication, harmony, purification, peace, prosperity, protection from dark powers, and communication with Earth energies and healing spirits. The American indigenous people believe connects the sky with the lakes.

Citrine Yellow

Citrine aids success, abundance, personal power, luck, generosity, happiness, mental clarity, and creativity. It is known as the Success Stone or Merchant's Stone.

Jasper Red and Orange

Red jasper aids in fairness, stabilization, protection, ancestral issues, responsibility, choice, and compassion. It is known as the Stone of Justice and the Stone of Controlled Passion. Orange jasper aids nurturing, gentleness, comfort, relaxation, prosperity, astral travel, protection, peace, enhancement of mental processes, and in balancing yin/yang energies. It is known as the Nurturing Stone.

Lapis Blue

Lapis aids awareness, prosperity, psychic abilities, truth, harmony, tranquility, expressiveness, cleansing, and in aligning the energy bodies.

Quartz Clear

Clear quartz is a universal stone that is a powerful transmitter. It aids in clarity, insight, perception, intention, and amplifying or directing energy. Since it is clear, it can be used for any intention. It is known as the All Healer.

Serpentine Yellow, Green, and Black

Serpentine comes in multiple colors. The photo shows a black stone. It aids emotional cleansing, psychic powers, protection, and attracts love and money. It is used in the rise of the kundalini and in meditation.

Sodalite Blue

Sodalite aids intelligence, knowledge, learning, logic, and truth. It is known as the Poet's Stone.

Rainbow Set of Stones

This set of seven stones is carved in the colors of the rainbow which also corresponds to the seven major Hindu *chakras* and the colors of the Cusco flag. In the set in the photo above, the round *hiwaya* stone has been added to represent zero. The colors of the rainbow can be remembered as the acronym ROY G BIV: **R**ed–**O**range–**Y**ellow **G**reen **B**lue–**I**ndigo–**V**iolet. The set usually consists of the following stones sourced from Peru: Red Jasper, Orange Jasper, Yellow Citrine, Green Chrysocolla, Blue Celestite, Blue Sodalite, and Purple Amethyst. This set is available at Sacred Pathways Marketplace (www.SacredPathways.us).

Chapter 2: Chumpi Stones 101   *17*

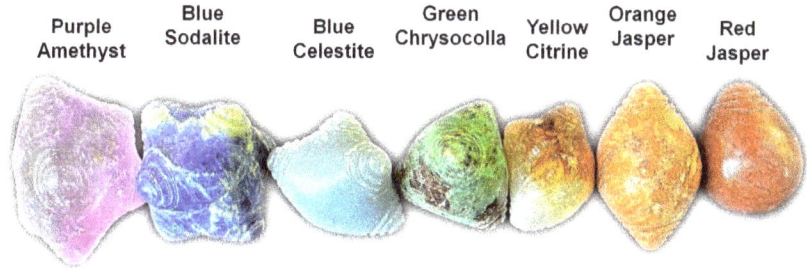

Trivia: The flag of Cusco is the rainbow flag of seven colors:

It is often mistaken for the LGBT+ rainbow flag, which only has six colors:

COLOR CORRESPONDENCES

The color correspondences of your *chumpi* set will be based on the material your set is carved from. Color modifies and directs energy. In general:

Warm and hot colors increase energy. (Reds, Oranges, Yellows)
Cool and cold colors decrease or absorb energy. (Blues, Indigos, Purples)
Earthy colors are neutral. (Greens, Golds, Silvers, and Black)
Greens and Browns represent the Physical Body.
Reds, Pinks, and Oranges represent the Emotional Body.
Blues, Indigos, and Yellows represent the Mental Body.
Purples, Golds, and Silvers represent the Spiritual Body.

Here are some correspondences associated with common colors:

Aqua or Turquoise (Blue Green)

Aqua or turquoise is blue-green. It corresponds with youth, speech, communication, confidence, strength, idealism, healing, and protection.

Black

Black is a master stone because it absorbs light that contains all colors. It corresponds with retribution, introspection, quietness, inner strength, energy absorption, protection, and the removal of bad vibrations.

Blue

Blue corresponds with health, peace, calm, intuition, inspiration, spirituality, happiness, kindness, psychic ability, compassion, energy absorption, and mental stimulation.

Brown

Brown corresponds with grounding, connection to Earth, justice, thrift, self-discipline, studiousness, and the practical.

Clear or Transparent

Stones that are clear or transparent are master stones because they contain all or none of the colors. They can be programmed with any intention.

Gray or Grey

Gray or grey corresponds with neutrality and developing self-knowledge.

Green

Green corresponds with money, luck, prosperity, business gain, abundance, fertility, success, new beginnings, hope, creativity, health, and healing.

Gold

Gold corresponds with prosperity, luck, fortune, new opportunities, honor, business gain, the Sun, and masculine energy.

Indigo

Indigo corresponds with intuition, seeking, beauty, and spirituality.

Orange

Orange corresponds with cheerfulness, concentration, optimism, hope, energy, recovering lost items, sexual and emotional stimulation.

Pink

Pink corresponds with friendship, love, tenderness, success, harmony, pleasure, loyalty, fortune, spiritual awakening, joy, and happiness.

Purple or Violet

Purple or violet is a perfect balance of hot and cold colors. It corresponds with success, career, mastery, courage, divination, exorcism, wisdom, dignity, spirituality, transition, death, royalty and soul development.

Trivia: Purple is also the perfect blend of red and blue, the traditional colors since World War Two that signify the feminine (red or pink) and masculine (blue) genders. This may be the reason that lavender or purple has become the color that represents gay identity.

Red

Red corresponds with love, romance, passion, attraction, affection, sex, lust, energy, strength, enthusiasm, and heat. In the Andes red represents *Pachamama* (Mother Earth) therefore, the Divine Feminine.

Silver

Silver corresponds with victory, goodness, money, power, development of the inner self, spirituality, the Moon, and feminine energy.

White

White corresponds with blessing, prayer, truth, purity, spiritual power, protection, cleansing, hope, harmony, peace, and healing. In the Andes, white represents the *Apukuna* (Mountain Spirits) therefore, the Divine Masculine.

Yellow

Yellow corresponds with luck, academic success, wisdom, concentration, cheerfulness, health, attractiveness, and removing hexes or bad luck.

NUMBER CORRESPONDENCES

All numbers have a unique energy and meaning in Numerology. The most distinguishing characteristic of the *chumpi* stone, other than its material, is the number of points it has. Below are the general correspondences for numbers zero through twelve:

Zero

Zero corresponds with the Void, the Source, infinite possibilities, all potential, and a blank slate.

One

One corresponds with beginnings, will, leadership, independence, and individual identity.

Two

Two corresponds with pairing, duality, balance, cooperation, peace, diplomacy, and complementary opposites.

Three

Three corresponds with creativity, self-expression, androgyny, the joining of two energies creates a third more powerful energy.

Four

4

Four corresponds with foundation, stability, organization, order, balance, wholeness, and work.

Five

5

Five corresponds with direction setting, freedom, versatility, change, resourcefulness, free will, experience, and representation of the human figure. Five is also the number of the Sacred Androgyne, a sum of the Triple Goddess and the Dual Horned God.

Six

6

Six corresponds with choices, multi-dimensions, responsibility, service, and beauty.

Seven

7

Seven corresponds with spiritual principles, expression, the Divine, detachment, harmony, wisdom, grace, and the place where spirit meets matter.

Eight

8

Eight corresponds with infinity, authority, power, knowledge, cause and effect (karma), recycling, equilibrium, and gaining mastery on all levels.

Nine

9

Nine corresponds with change, altruism, compassion, universal love, hierarchy, completion of a cycle, returning to a new beginning.

Ten

10

Ten corresponds with new life, marriage, releasing the old, and accepting the new.

Eleven

11

Eleven corresponds with intuition, the unknown, and the acceptance of what has been as well as what will be. Eleven is the first of three "Master Numbers" and it represents the first phase of creation, the Visionary.

Twelve

12

Twelve corresponds with order, mastery, and opening to Divine Powers.

TEXTILE CORRESPONDENCES

The Q'ero and other indigenous Andean people weave textiles in their mountain villages. Each village has a unique style and color palette unique to its community. Textiles are usually woven on backstrap looms. They are created from the natural fibers of alpaca, sheep, and llama. They are then dyed and spun into threads. Lastly, they are hand woven into beautiful patterns. Weaving consists of two threads: warp is the longitudinal or the vertical thread and weft (also woof) is the transverse or horizontal thread. A single thread of the weft, crossing the warp, is called a pick. There are two main energetics woven into the textiles. The solid colors, called "*pampa*", are a place of rest. The threads that create a pattern, called "*pallay*", create energetic movement.

All of the patterns woven into Andean textiles have meaning, intention, and represent the energetic universe. The Andean people place great value on their textiles. They serve practical purposes such as blankets, shawls, ponchos, pouches, ropes, hats, and belts but they also hold a symbolic presence in the lives and ceremonies of the people. The energetic vibrations of the textiles increase through their interlacing fibers, patterns, and the intentions of the weavers as they are created. Following is the correspondence of the textile design that best fits the energy of the *chumpi* stone numbers from zero to twelve.

For a more in-depth exploration of Andean textiles, these books provide great references:

Textile Traditions of Chinchero: A Living Heritage by Nilda Callañaupa Alvarez

Weaving in the Peruvian Highlands: Dreaming Patterns, Weaving Memories by Nilda Callañaupa Alvarez

Hidden Threads of Peru: Q'ero Textiles by Ann Pollard Rowe and John Cohen

A Woven Book of Knowledge: Textile Iconography of Cuzco, Peru by Gail P. Silverman

0 Pampa

Pampa is an expanse of flat land. In a textile, the blocks of solid color are called "*pampa*" The space of pattern-less solid color provides a place of rest and calm energy. *Pampa* is used to represent zero because there is an absence of pattern yet it holds all the possibilities of creation. *Pampa* within a cloth represents the Unmanifest. Its solid color without a design can provide calming energy.

1 Ch'unchu

 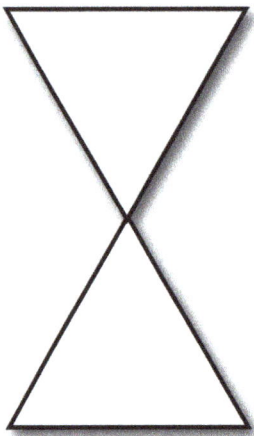 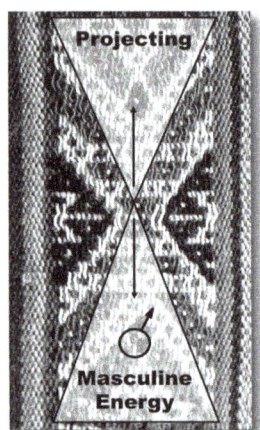

The *ch'unchu* (wild indigenous soul) is a representation of a mythical native jungle dancer, who came from the lowland rainforest and wore a very tall feather headdress. It is woven as an hourglass shape of legs and body projecting toward the ground and arms and head projecting toward the sky. The *ch'unchu* represents self-identity, our origin, projecting or activating energy, and is the intermediary between earth and sky. The upper half of *ch'unchu* represents the *hananpacha*: the above, the masculine, and the right hand. The lower half represents the *hurinpacha*: the below, the feminine, and the left hand. The *ch'unchu* figure represents personal identity. It can be used to connect to the energy of your origin and personal roots.

2 Iskay (2-Panel) Cloth

The 2-panel cloth consists of two solid colors in one textile. It represents reciprocity, relationship, and all complementary pairs. The 2-panel cloth represents duality and complimentary pairs. Its solid colors without any pattern can provide calming energy.

Chapter 2: Chumpi Stones 101

3 Apu

 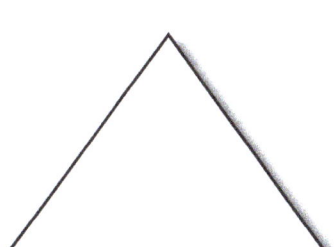 

The *apu* (sacred mountain) is one of the most revered symbols to the Andean indigenous people. They are surrounded by mountains where they live. These mountains are the closest places to the stars on Earth. Each of the Q'ero has a particular peak from which they source. The *apu* also represents the triangle. **Note:** This symbol can also be interpreted as the rising (left photo) or setting sun (right photo). The *apu* on a cloth can represent movement. This symbol can provide a link between the terrestrial and the celestial.

4 Tawantinsuyu (4-Panel) Cloth

The *Tawantinsuyu* is the four regions of the Inka Empire. (The *Tawantinsuyu* is illustrated in the Appendix on page 110 and 111.) *Tawantin* is also the harmonic union of four separate energies. The inclusion of all parts makes the whole stronger. A 4-panel cloth consists of four solid colors in one textile. It represents foundation and stability. The 4-panel cloth represents foundation. It can be used to connect to the energies of organization and stabilization.

5 Chakana Cloth

The *chakana* cloth is a graphical interpretation of the Southern Cross star constellation only seen from the Southern Hemisphere. It is also referred to as the Andean Cross, Inka Cross, the Southern Star, and the Stairway. The *chakana* is a design that reflects many of the Q'ero cosmological concepts. The hole through the center is a portal to other dimensions. The *chakana* represents orienting, navigation, and guidance. The *chakana* cloth is representative of orientation. It can be used to connect to the energy of direction-finding and connecting to the celestial.

6 Ñawi

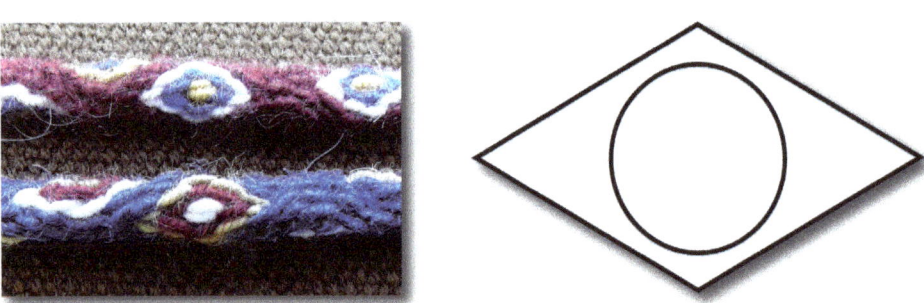

Woven *ñawi* (eyes) usually appear as patterned cords or as borders on textiles. The *ñawi* design outlines, protects, and enhances the woven energy field that lies within. The *ñawi* on a cloth is the representation of relationships. They can be used to connect to the energy of clear vision.

7 K'uychi

The *k'uychi* or *k'uichi* (rainbow) is a symbol woven into Andean cloth that includes all the colors of the rainbow. The rainbow appears quite often in Q'ero cosmology as a symbol of participation and the expression of all possibility. The rainbow is a bridge between the natural and supernatural worlds. It represents unity, the rainbow light body, the divine pathway, and the full expression of light. A *k'uychi* on a cloth is representative of expression. It can be used to connect to the energies of inclusivity, diversity, or balance.

8 Tawa Inti Qocha

 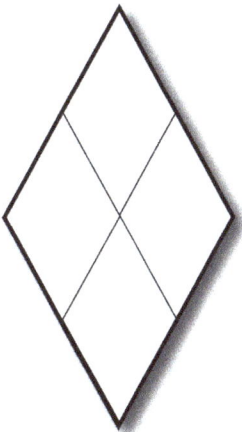 

Similar to the *inti* design, *tawa inti qocha* (Four Sun Lake) is a diamond composed of four smaller diamonds that represent the four aspects of daily time (sunrise, noon, sunset, and midnight) and the four seasons of the year (spring, summer, fall, and winter). Dark lines touching the main diamond's outline signify the setting sun. Lighter lines that do not touch the main diamond's outline but instead touch the rectangular frame, signify a rising sun. The *tawa inti qocha* symbol is representative of infinity. It can be used to connect to the energies of the cycles of time.

9 Inti

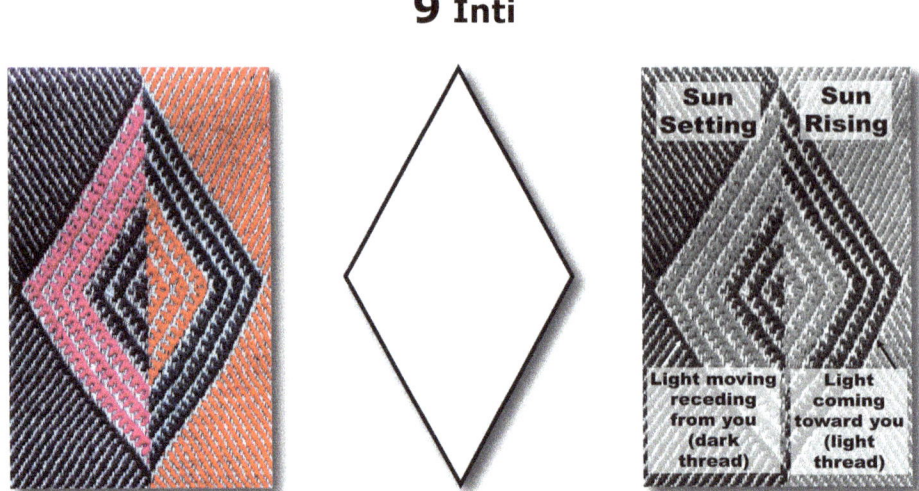

Version 1: One Diamond Sun with sunrise on one side and sunset on the other side.

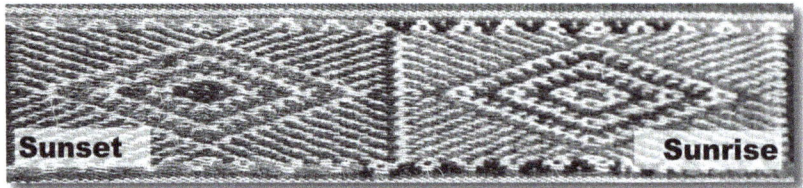

Version 2: Two Diamond Suns, one with sunrising and one with sunsetting.

Inti (sun) is depicted as a diamond shape with straight lines representing the sun's rays radiating to and from the edge of a diamond. The vertical center line signifies the center of village, the sun at zenith, and the Milky Way. Dark rays and borders are the sun setting. Light rays and borders are the sun rising. The inti symbol is representative of completion. It can be used to connect to the masculine energy or to illuminate a particular issue or idea.

Inti Chinkapushan are dark colored lines touching the diamond's outline that signify dusk, shadow, and light falling or receding from the viewer. *Inti Lloqsimushan* are light colored lines touching the diamond's outline that signify dawn, sunlight, and light lifting or advancing toward the viewer.

10 Ch'ily Qocha

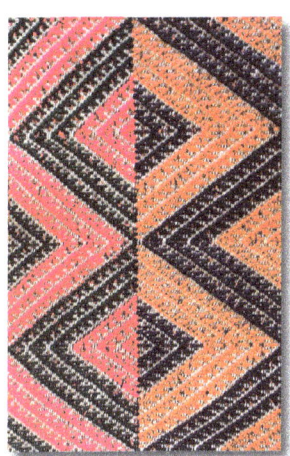 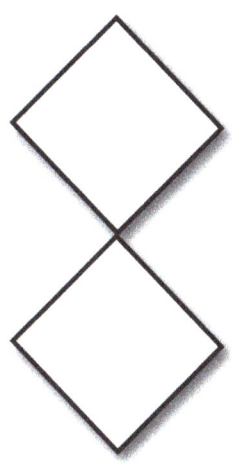 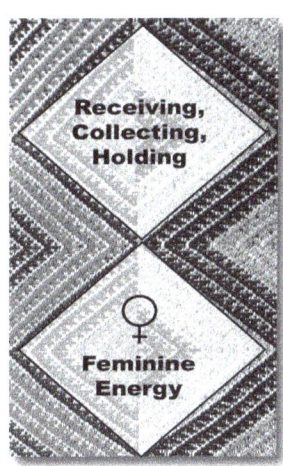

Ch'ily qocha is composed of symmetrical zig zags of diamonds usually in contrasting colors. *Qocha* means body of water, lake, pool, or pond. *Ch'ili* is a type of grass in the Andes that is important to the llamas and alpacas. The *ch'ily qocha* pattern is a diamond shape whose lines hold rather than radiate out as in the *inti* or *ch'unchu* designs. Since *qocha* is a place for holding water, it can be considered a feminine symbol of the womb of creation. The *ch'ily qocha* symbol is representative of rebirth. It can be used to connect to feminine energy or to give fluidity to an issue or idea.

11 Pallay

Pallay is the sacred patterns on the cloth which hold energetic signatures. *Pallay* literally means "to pick up," in this case picking up threads among the warp. The *pallay* directs energy to and from the cloth, thus forming an energetic grid. *Pallay* is on a textile is representative of balance. It can be used to stir up or move energy.

12 Pallay Tukuy

The *pallay tukuy* (finishing design) is the rough patch toward the end of a textile. It occurs in a backstrap weaving and must be hand-sewn in a more loose or formless way as a transition from one part of the fabric to another. It is sometimes mistaken to be an error in the weaving but this can be considered the place that the weaver's soul leaves the piece at completion. The *pallay tukuy* is representative of mastery, the great finish. It can be used to connect to the energy of finishing a project or issue.

CHAPTER 3

CHUMPI STONE CORRESPONDENCES

CHUMPI STONES BY THE NUMBERS

This chapter gives correspondences for the *chumpi* stones numbers from zero to twelve. Robert Wakeley Wheeler (my co-author of *The Chakana Oracle Guidebook* and card deck) and I began the correspondences for *chumpi* stones zero to seven together. Subsequently, I added to the correspondences for these and then added the correspondences for stones eight through twelve. These correspondences are based on my personal research and experiences with the Q'ero cosmology. You may choose to go by this text or develop your own with the symbolism that has evolved from your personal experiences. Creating correspondences is about setting intentions so that energy will follow where attention focuses it.

Chumpi stones hold multiple energies including: the energy of the stone itself, the energy of the number of protrusions on the stone, the energy of the symbol carved on the stone, the energy of its sacred geometric form, the energy of the Pleiades, the energy of the *apu* (mountain spirit) the stone is connected to, and the cultural associations of the originator as well as the user.

Following, is a detailed description for each number from zero to twelve. At the end of this chapter, you will find a summary chart of the correspondences.

Note: Even though *chumpi* stones come from Andean culture, the following correspondences are sourced from multiple cultures including Pagan, Celtic, Hindu, as well as North and South Native American. The Western world has become a cultural melting pot and thus has a multitude of esoteric beliefs originating from many spiritual traditions. There are individuals that have a purist viewpoint that spiritual and cultural attributes should never be mixed. There are other individuals that have an eclectic viewpoint, which includes combining bits from many traditions. It is up to you to take what you will from these correspondences, leave what you don't want, and add whatever you feel is missing.

There is a worksheet in the Appendix on page 108 that can be used to document the correspondences for your *chumpi* stone set. This worksheet is also available as a download at www.ChumpiSacredStones.com.

Chapter 3: Chumpi Stone Correspondences 35

NUMBER: CH'USAQ (ZERO)

Note: Carved *chumpi* stone sets do not come with zero points, however, the *chumpi* stone owner can add a marble or other circular object to represent zero, to their set. Some will feel it not necessary to represent zero and some will like to recognize zero.

NUMBER OF POINTS: *Ch'usaq K'uchu* (Zero Point)

GRAPHICAL REPRESENTATIONS:

GEOMETRIC SHAPE: Circle

SYMBOLISM: The Unmanifest

CHAKRA: Earth Star (Three feet below the feet)

COLOR: *Q'ispi kay* (Transparent)

ANDEAN ARCHETYPE: None

ANDEAN TEXTILE DESIGN: *Pampa* or *Chacra* (Field)

ANDEAN GODDESS: None

APU (Mountain): None

SAPA INKA: None

DIRECTION: None

CELESTIAL BODY: Chiron, The Wounded Healer

WESTERN ASTROLOGICAL HOUSE: None

WESTERN ZODIAC ARCHETYPE: Ophiuchus, The Man Grasping a Snake

CHINESE ZODIAC ARCHETYPE: None

TAROT CARD: The Fool

WESTERN ELEMENT: None

CHINESE ELEMENT: None

KINGDOM: None

TIME OF THE DAY: None

SEASON OF THE YEAR: None

HUMAN ASPECT: None

COMMUNITY CONSCIOUSNESS: None

HUMAN AGE: *Yumay* (Conception)

CYCLE OF LIFE: None

PAGAN HOLIDAY (Northern Hemisphere Wheel of the Year): None

PAGAN HOLIDAY (Southern Hemisphere Wheel of the Year): None

DAY OF THE WEEK: None

MONTH OF THE YEAR: None

PERSONALITY: Absolute, All and Nothing, Beginner, Birthing, Blank Slate, Infinite Possibility, Mystery, Neutral, Nothingness, Oneness, Open, Potential, Undefined, Unmanifest, Void

COSMOLOGY:

Mama Tuta (The Dark Void)

Wiracocha Inti (Source, Creator/Creatress; God/Goddess, Great Spirit)

NUMBER: HUQ (ONE)

NUMBER OF POINTS: *Huq K'uchu Rumi* (One Point Stone) aka *Ch'ulla* (Single Foot)

GRAPHICAL REPRESENTATIONS:

GEOMETRIC SHAPE Dot (Single Point)

SYMBOLISM: Personal Identity

CHAKRA: 1st Root, Survival

COLOR: *Puka* (Red)

ANDEAN ARCHETYPE: *Sach'amama* or *Amaru* (Serpent or Snake)

ANDEAN TEXTILE DESIGN: *Ch'unchu* (Indigenous Jungle Dancer)

ANDEAN GODDESS: Mama Ocllo represents Pachamama (Goddess of the Earth). She is wife and sister of Manco Cápac, founder of Cusco and the Inka lineage.

APU (Mountain): Ausangate

SAPA INKA: Manco Cápac (Manqo Qhapaq) Ruled in early 1200s

DIRECTION: *Uray* (South)

CELESTIAL BODY: Mars

WESTERN ASTROLOGICAL HOUSE: 1 House of Identity

WESTERN ZODIAC ARCHETYPE: Aries, The Ram

CHINESE ZODIAC ARCHETYPE: Rat

TAROT CARD: Magician / Medicine Man

WESTERN ELEMENT: *Nina* (Fire)

CHINESE ELEMENT: *Nina* (Fire)

KINGDOM: *Qiqlla* (Mineral)

TIME OF THE DAY: *Punchayay* (Sunrise)

SEASON OF THE YEAR: *Chiraw mit'a* (Spring)

HUMAN ASPECT: Body

COMMUNITY CONSCIOUSNESS: *Ayllu* (Family or Village)

HUMAN AGE: *Wachakuy* (Birth)

CYCLE OF LIFE: Seed

PAGAN HOLIDAY (Northern Hemisphere Wheel of the Year): None

PAGAN HOLIDAY (Southern Hemisphere Wheel of the Year): None

DAY OF THE WEEK: *Killa chaw* (Monday) Oneday

MONTH OF THE YEAR: *Iniru killa* (January)

PERSONALITY: Ambition, Focus, Independence, Pioneer, Root, Scout, Self-Consciousness, Self-sufficiency, Singular Conscious Awareness. Single, Unique

COSMOLOGY:

Ch'ulla (Single Foot, Monocot)

Ch'unchu (Indigenous Jungle Dancer)

Huaca (Place of Sacred Power)

NUMBER: ISKAY (TWO)

NUMBER OF POINTS: *Iskay K'uchu Rumi* (Two Point Stone) aka *Yanantin* (harmonious relationship of dissimilar energies)

GRAPHICAL REPRESENTATIONS:

GEOMETRIC SHAPE: Line (line between two points) ———

SYMBOLISM: Duality (Complementary Pairs)

CHAKRA: 2nd Sacral, Creativity and Sexuality

COLOR: *Wallapi* (Orange)

ANDEAN ARCHETYPE: *Puma* (Cougar); *Otorongo* or *Chinchay* (Jaguar) For clarification see notes on *Otorongo* in the glossary.

ANDEAN TEXTILE DESIGN: *Iskay* (2-panel) Cloth

ANDEAN GODDESS: Doña Mujia, the Mermaid, is the Goddess of the Water

APU (Mountain): Salkantay

SAPA INKA: Sinchi Roca (Zinchi Roq'a) Ruled in 1230s

DIRECTION: *Intiq Iluqsinan* (West)

CELESTIAL BODY: Venus

WESTERN ASTROLOGICAL HOUSE: 2 House of Value and Self Worth

WESTERN ZODIAC ARCHETYPE: Taurus, The Bull

CHINESE ZODIAC ARCHETYPE: Ox

TAROT CARD: High Priestess / Medicine Woman

WESTERN ELEMENT: *Allpa* (Earth)

CHINESE ELEMENT: *Allpa* (Earth)

KINGDOM: *Qora* (Plant)

TIME OF THE DAY: *Chawpidiya* (Noon)

SEASON OF THE YEAR: *Ruphay mit'a* (Summer)

HUMAN ASPECT: Emotions

COMMUNITY CONSCIOUSNESS: *Llaqta* (City)

HUMAN AGE: *Wawa* (Childhood)

CYCLE OF LIFE: Germinate

PAGAN HOLIDAY (Northern Hemisphere Wheel of the Year): Imbolc

PAGAN HOLIDAY (Southern Hemisphere Wheel of the Year): Lughnasadh

DAY OF THE WEEK: *Ati chaw* (Tuesday) Twosday

MONTH OF THE YEAR: *Hiwriru killa* (February)

PERSONALITY: Adaptable, Aligned, Altered, Balance, Community Consciousness, Complement, Contrast, Cooperation, Couple, Dualistic Conscious Awareness, Opposite, Pair, Partner

COSMOLOGY: Complementary Pairs of:

Ch'aki (Dry) and *Api* (Wet)

Chiri (Cold) and *Qoñi* (Warm)

Hanan (Upper) and *Hurin* (Lower)

Hapu (Union of two harmonized *yanantin*, dissimilar, energies) and *Ranti* (Union of two harmonized *masintin*, similar, energies)

Hawa (Outside, Outer) and *Ukhu* (Inside, Inner)

Huaca (Place of energy) and *Ceque* (Energy lines)

Inka (Son of the Sun) and *Qoya* (Queen)

Inkari (Inka) and *Collari* (Wife of Inka)

Inti Tayta (Father Sun) and *Mama Killa* (Mother Moon)

Itu (Masculine Nature Spirit) and *Pacarino* (Feminine Nature Spirit)

K'anchay (Luminous Energy) and *Kawsay* (Life Force Energy)

Lirpuy (Reflect) and *Ukyay* (?) Absorb

Llank'i (Smooth) and *Qhasqa* (Rough)

Mink'a (Need) and *Mit'a* (Service)

Mu (Coming Toward) and *Pu* (Moving Away)

Pa (Calm) and *Cha* (Active) (From *Pacha*, spacetime)

Paña (Right) and *Lloq'e* (Left)

Pallay (Pattern) and *Pampa* (Plain)

Pipu (Thick) and *Harchi* (Thin)

Puka (Red) and *Yuraq* (White)

Punchay (Day) and *Tuta* (Night)

Qhari (Man) and *Warmi* (Woman)

Qocha (Collection) and *Ch'unchu* (Projection)

Saiwachakuy (Column Energy Earth to Heaven) and *Saminchakuy* (Silo Energy Heaven to Earth)

Sami (High Vibratory Energy) and *Hucha* (Heavy Energy)

Wachakuy (Birth) and *Wañuy* (Death)

Yanantin (Relationship between opposite energies) and *Masintin* (Relationship between similar energies)

NUMBER: KINSA (THREE)

NUMBER OF POINTS: *Kinsa K'uchu Rumi* (Three Point Stone) aka *Kinsantin*

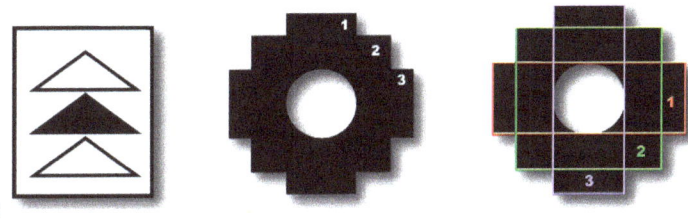

GRAPHICAL REPRESENTATIONS:

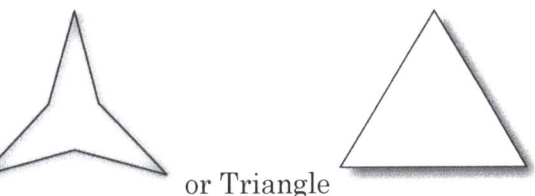

GEOMETRIC SHAPE: 3-pointed Star or Triangle

SYMBOLISM: Movement

CHAKRA: 3rd Solar Plexus, Power Center

COLOR: *Q'ello* (Yellow)

ANDEAN ARCHETYPE: *Siwar Q'enti* (Royal Hummingbird)

ANDEAN TEXTILE DESIGN: *Apu* (Mountain)

ANDEAN GODDESS: Mama Simona, the oldest feminine mountain in Peru, is the Goddess of Origin and Our Ancestors

APU (Mountain): Pachatusan

SAPA INKA: Lloque Yupanqui (Lloqe Yupanki) Ruled in 1260s

DIRECTION: *Chincha* (North)

CELESTIAL BODY: Mercury

WESTERN ASTROLOGICAL HOUSE: 3 House of Communications

WESTERN ZODIAC ARCHETYPE: Gemini

CHINESE ZODIAC ARCHETYPE: Tiger

TAROT CARD: Empress / Grandmother

WESTERN ELEMENT: *Wayra* (Air)

CHINESE ELEMENT: *Q'illay* (Metal)

KINGDOM: *Uywa* (Animal)

TIME OF THE DAY: *Ch'isiyay* (Sunset)

SEASON OF THE YEAR: *Puquy mit'a* (Autumn)

HUMAN ASPECT: Mind

COMMUNITY CONSCIOUSNESS: *Suyu* (Region or Nation)

HUMAN AGE: *Warma* (Adolescence)

CYCLE OF LIFE: Grow

PAGAN HOLIDAY (Northern Hemisphere Wheel of the Year): Ostara, Spring Equinox

PAGAN HOLIDAY (Southern Hemisphere Wheel of the Year): Mabon, Autumn Equinox

DAY OF THE WEEK: *Qoyllur chaw* (Wednesday)

MONTH OF THE YEAR: *Marsu killa* (March)

PERSONALITY: Break Out, Connected with Ancestors, Dimensional, Dynamic, Growth, Human Consciousness, Social, Synthesize, Unity Conscious Awareness

COSMOLOGY:

    Three Shamanic Worlds: *Ukhupacha* (Lower World), *Kaypacha* (Middle World), and *Hanaqpacha* (Upper World)

    Three Archetypes: *Sach'amama* (Serpent or Snake of the Lower World), *Puma* or *Otorongo* (Cougar or Jaguar of the Middle World), and *Hatun Kuntur* (Condor of the Upper World)

    Three Dimensions of Time: *Unaypacha* (Past), *Kunanpacha* (Present), and *Hamaqpacha* (Future)

    Three Camelids: Llama, Alpaca, and Vicua

    Three Directions: *Paña* (Right), *Lloq'e* (Left), and *Chawpin* (Center)

    Three Golden Rules of the Inka: *Ama suway* (Do not steal), *Ama qella* (Do not be lazy), and *Ama Llulla* (Do not lie)

    Three Intentions: *Yachay* (Right Thought), *Munay* (Right Intention), and *Llank'ay* (Right Action)

    Three Primary Energies: *Kawsay* (Life Force Energy), *Sami* (High Vibratory Energy), *K'anchay* (Luminous Energy)

    Three Relationships: *Mink'a* (Need), *Mit'a* (Service), and *Ayni* (Reciprocity)

    Three steps of the *Chakana* (The Southern Cross star constellation)

    K'intu (Group of three coca leaves used for sacred purposes)

Chapter 3: Chumpi Stone Correspondences 43

NUMBER: TAWA (FOUR)

NUMBER OF POINTS: *Tawa K'uchu Rumi* (Four Point Stone) aka *Tawantin*

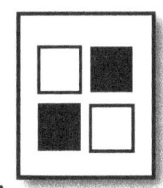 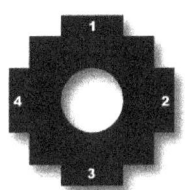

GRAPHICAL REPRESENTATIONS:

GEOMETRIC SHAPE: 4-pointed Star   or Square

SYMBOLISM: Foundation

CHAKRA: 4th Heart, Love

COLOR: *Q'omer* (Green)

ANDEAN ARCHETYPE: *Kuntur* (Condor)

ANDEAN TEXTILE DESIGN: *Tawantinsuyu* (4-panel) Cloth

ANDEAN GODDESS: Doña Theresa, a heart shaped mountain in the Sacred Valley, is the Goddess of Love and Harmony

APU (Mountain): Huanacauri

SAPA INKA: Mayta Cápac (Mayta Qhapaq) Ruled in 1290s

DIRECTION: *Intiq Iluqsinan* (East)

CELESTIAL BODY: Moon

WESTERN ASTROLOGICAL HOUSE: 4 House of Home and Family

WESTERN ZODIAC ARCHETYPE: Cancer

CHINESE ZODIAC ARCHETYPE: Rabbit

TAROT CARD: Emperor / Grandfather

WESTERN ELEMENT: *Unu* (Water)

CHINESE ELEMENT: *Unu* (Water)

KINGDOM: *Runa* (Human)

TIME OF THE DAY: *Khuskantuta* (Midnight)

SEASON OF THE YEAR: *Chiri mit'a* (Winter)

HUMAN ASPECT: Spirit

COMMUNITY CONSCIOUSNESS: *Teqse* (Global)

HUMAN AGE: *Sayaqruna* (Adulthood)

CYCLE OF LIFE: Bud

PAGAN HOLIDAY (Northern Hemisphere Wheel of the Year): None

PAGAN HOLIDAY (Southern Hemisphere Wheel of the Year): None

DAY OF THE WEEK: *Illapa chaw* (Thursday) Foursday

MONTH OF THE YEAR: *Awril killa* (April)

PERSONALITY: Building, Divine Consciousness, Down-to-earth, Formation, Ground, Order, Organization, Practical, Secure, Solid, Spatial, Stable, Steady

COSMOLOGY:

    Four Cardinal Directions: *Chincha* (North), *Intiq Iluqsinan* (East), *Uray* (South), and *Intiq Chinkanan* (West)

    Four Colors of the Tawantinsuyu: *Q'omer* (Green), *Yuraq* (White), *Q'ello* (Yellow), and *Puka* (Red)

    Four Directions of the *Tawantinsuyu* (Inka Empire): *Antisuyu* (NE), *Qollasuyu* (SE), *Kuntisuyu* (SW), and *Chinchaysuyu* (NW)

    Four Elements: *Allpa* (Earth), *Unu* (Water), *Wayra* (Wind), and *Nina* (Fire)

    Four Seasons: *Puquy mit'a* (Autumn), *Chiri mit'a* (Winter), *Chiraw mit'a* (Spring), and *Ruphay mit'a* (Summer)

    Four Sides or Points of the *Chakana* (The Southern Cross star constellation)

    Four Phases of Moon: *Killawañuy* (New), *Killapura* (Full), Waxing Quarter, Waning Quarter

Chapter 3: Chumpi Stone Correspondences 45

NUMBER: PISQA (FIVE)

NUMBER OF POINTS: *Pisqa K'uchu Rumi* (Five Point Stone) aka *Pisqantin*

GRAPHICAL REPRESENTATIONS: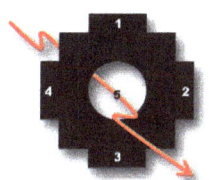

 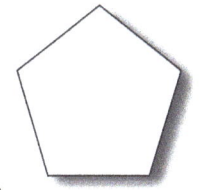

GEOMETRIC SHAPE: 5-sided Star or Pentagon

SYMBOLISM: Orientation

CHAKRA: 5th Throat, Expression

COLOR: *Anqas* (Blue)

ANDEAN ARCHETYPE: *Chakana* (The Southern Cross star constellation)

ANDEAN TEXTILE DESIGN: *Chakana* Cloth

ANDEAN GODDESS: Maria Sakapana is the Goddess of the Wind and Communication

APU (Mountain): Saqsaywaman

SAPA INKA: Cápac Yupanki (Qhapaq Yupanki) Ruled in 1320s

DIRECTION: *Antisuyu* (Northeast)

CELESTIAL BODY: Sun

WESTERN ASTROLOGICAL HOUSE: 5 House of Pleasure and Creativity

WESTERN ZODIAC ARCHETYPE: Leo

CHINESE ZODIAC ARCHETYPE: Dragon

TAROT CARD: Hierophant / Shaman

WESTERN ELEMENT: *Nuna* (Spirit)

CHINESE ELEMENT: *Qiru* (Wood)

TIME OF THE DAY: None

SEASON OF THE YEAR: None

HUMAN ASPECT: None

COMMUNITY CONSCIOUSNESS: *Ch'askakancha* (Universal)

HUMAN AGE: *Chawpipacha* (Middle Age)

CYCLE OF LIFE: Bloom

PAGAN HOLIDAY (Northern Hemisphere Wheel of the Year): Beltane

PAGAN HOLIDAY (Southern Hemisphere Wheel of the Year): Samhain

DAY OF THE WEEK: *Ch'aska chaw* (Friday)

MONTH OF THE YEAR: *Mayu killa* (May)

PERSONALITY: Center, Direction Setting, Navigational Guide, Orientation, Planetary Consciousness

COSMOLOGY:

Five *Chumpi* (Belt) Bands: *Yana Chumpi* (Black Belt), *Puka Chumpi* (Red Belt), *Qori Chumpi* (Gold Belt), *Qolqe Chumpi* (Silver Belt), and *Kulli Chumpi* (Violet Belt)

Five Directions of the *Chakana* (The Southern Cross star constellation): The four cardinal directions plus the center portal

Five Directions of the Suyu: *Antisuyu* (Northeast), *Qollasuyu* (Southeast), *Kuntisuyu* (Southwest), *Chinchaysuyu* (Northwest), and *Chawpinsuyu* (Center)

Five Elements: *Allpa* (Earth), *Unu* (Water), *Wayra* (Wind), *Nina* (Fire), and *Nuna* (Spirit-Ether)

Five Levels of Community Consciousness: *Ayllu* (Family or Village), *Llaqta* (City), *Suyu* (Regional or National), *Teqse* (Global), and *Ch'askakancha* (Universal)

NUMBER: SUQTA (SIX)

NUMBER OF POINTS: *Suqta K'uchu Rumi* (Six Point Stone) aka *Suqtatin*

GRAPHICAL REPRESENTATIONS:

 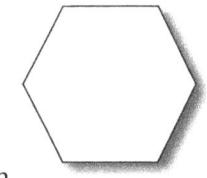

GEOMETRIC SHAPE: 6-pointed Star   or Hexagon

SYMBOLISM: Relationship

CHAKRA: 6th Third Eye, Perception, *Yanchay*

COLOR: *Tinaku Ilimphi* (Indigo)

ANDEAN ARCHETYPE: *Mama Killa* (Mother Moon)

ANDEAN TEXTILE DESIGN: *Ñawi* (Eyes)

ANDEAN GODDESS: Doña Juana (Huana) Waman (Falcon) Tiklla is the Goddess of Vision

APU (Mountain): Huacawilka

SAPA INKA: Inka Roca (Inka Roq'a) Ruled in 1350s

DIRECTION: *Qollasuyu* (Southeast)

CELESTIAL BODY: Juno, Pallas, and Vesta

WESTERN ASTROLOGICAL HOUSE: 6 House of Health and Service

WESTERN ZODIAC ARCHETYPE: Virgo

CHINESE ZODIAC ARCHETYPE: Snake

TAROT CARD: Lovers

WESTERN ELEMENT: None

CHINESE ELEMENT: None

TIME OF THE DAY: None

SEASON OF THE YEAR: None

HUMAN ASPECT: None

COMMUNITY CONSCIOUSNESS: None

HUMAN AGE: *Machuyasqa* (male) and *Payayasqa* (female) Elderhood

CYCLE OF LIFE: Mature

PAGAN HOLIDAY (Northern Hemisphere Wheel of the Year): Litha, Summer Solstice

PAGAN HOLIDAY (Southern Hemisphere Wheel of the Year): Yule, Winter Solstice, *Inti Raymi* (Inka Sun Festival)

DAY OF THE WEEK: *K'uychi chaw* (Saturday)

MONTH OF THE YEAR: *Huniyu killa* (June)

PERSONALITY: Co-creation, Cosmic Consciousness, Receptivity, Harmony, Integration, Relation, Universal Conscious Awareness

COSMOLOGY:

- Six Andean Qualities: *Yachay* (Right Thought), *Munay* (Right Intention), *Llank'ay* (Right Action), *Ayni* (Right Relationship), *Kawsay* (Life Force Energy), and *Allyu* (Community)

- Six States of Energy: *Sami* (High Vibratory), *Hucha* (Heavy), *Poq'po* (Bubble), *Huaca* (Sacred Vortex), *Ceque* (Line of Energy) and *Kawsay* (Life Force)

- Six Dimensions: *Hanaqpacha* (Upper), *Kaypacha* (Middle), and *Ukhupacha* (Lower) plus *Ñawpapacha* (Past), *Kunanpacha* (Present), and *Qhipapacha* (Future)

Chapter 3: Chumpi Stone Correspondences 49

NUMBER: QANCHIS (SEVEN)

NUMBER OF POINTS: *Qanchis K'uchu Rumi* (Seven Point Stone) aka *Qanchistin*

GRAPHICAL REPRESENTATIONS:

GEOMETRIC SHAPE: 7-pointed Star   or Heptagon

SYMBOLISM: Expression

CHAKRA: 7th Crown, Spirit, Soul

COLOR: *Kulli* (Violet)

ANDEAN ARCHETYPE: *Inti Tayta* (Father Sun)

ANDEAN TEXTILE DESIGN: *K'uychi* (Rainbow)

ANDEAN GODDESS: Doña Tomasa Waman (Falcon) Tiklla is the Goddess of Freedom, Inner Silence and Non-attachment

APU (Mountain): Machu Picchu

SAPA INKA: Yahuár Huacác (Yawar Waqaq) Ruled in 1380s

DIRECTION: *Kuntisuyu* (Southwest)

CELESTIAL BODY: Ceres

WESTERN ASTROLOGICAL HOUSE: 7 House of Relationships and Partnerships

WESTERN ZODIAC ARCHETYPE: Libra

CHINESE ZODIAC ARCHETYPE: Horse

TAROT CARD: Chariot / Spiritual Warrior

WESTERN ELEMENT: None

CHINESE ELEMENT: None

TIME OF THE DAY: None

SEASON OF THE YEAR: None

HUMAN ASPECT: None

COMMUNITY CONSCIOUSNESS: None

HUMAN AGE: *Wañuy* (Death)

CYCLE OF LIFE: Wilt

PAGAN HOLIDAY (Northern Hemisphere Wheel of the Year): None

PAGAN HOLIDAY (Southern Hemisphere Wheel of the Year): None

DAY OF THE WEEK: *Apu chaw* (Sunday)

MONTH OF THE YEAR: *Huliyu killa* (July)

PERSONALITY: Connected to Source, Enlightenment, Expression, Introspection, Esoteric Knowledge, Magic, Multiverse Consciousness, Mysticism, Spirit, Wisdom

COSMOLOGY:

Seven Colors of Cusco Flag and the Rainbow: *Puka* (Red), *Wallapi* (Orange), *Q'ello* (Yellow), *Q'omir* (Green), *Qosi* (Light Blue), *Anqas* (Royal Blue), and *Kulli* (Violet)

Seven Directions in Space: *Hawa* (Above), *Ura* (Below), *Paña* (Right), *L'loqe* (Left), *Qhepa* (Behind), *Ñawpa* (Before), and *Ukhu* (Within)

Seven *Inka Ñawi* (Energy Eyes): *Siki Ñawi* (Tail Eye), *Qosqo Ñawi* (Belly Eye), *Sonqo Ñawi* (Heart Eye), *Kunka Ñawi* (Throat Eye), *Paña Ñawi* (Right Eye), *Lkoq'e Ñawi* (Left Eye), and *Qanchis Ñawi* (Seven Eye)

Seven Layers of the *Saiwa Kawsay* (Life Force): *Kallari* (Flow-Change), *Ch'ulla* (Oneness), *Yachay* (Wisdom), *Cheqaq* (Truth), *Nuna* (Spirit-Soul), and *Munay* (Love)

Seven *Ñust'a* (Female Spirits): Mama Ocllo, Dona Mujia, Mama Simona, Doña Theresa, Maria Sakapana, Doña Juana (Huana) Waman Tiklla, Doña Tomasa Waman Tiklla

Seven Principles of the Living Energy World (from work of Juan del Prado): *Kawsay Pacha* (Living Energy), *Ayni* (Sacred Exchange), *Yanantin* (Harmonious Relationship), *Inka Muju* (Energy Seed), *Karpay* (Energy Transmission), *Wiñay* (Energy Germination), and *Phutuy* (Energy Flowering)

Seven Sisters of the *Qotokuna* (Pleiades): *Puriq qoto* (Asterope/Sterope 1 and 2), *Tarpuq qoto* (Taygeta), *Ñawi qoto* (Maia), *Munay qoto* (Celeano), *Llank'aq qoto* (Electra), *Yllari qoto* (Merope), and *K'anchaq qoto* (Alcyone)

Seven Levels of Andean Psychospiritual Development (from work of Juan Nuñez del Prado): *Paq'o* (1st Level), *Pampa Misayoc* (2nd Level), *Alto Misayoc* (3rd Level), *Kuraq Akulleq* (4th Level), *Inka Mallku* and *Ñust'a* (5th Level), *Sapa Inka* and *Qoya* (6th Level), and *Taytanchis Ranti* (7th Level)

Chapter 3: Chumpi Stone Correspondences 51

NUMBER: PUSAQ (EIGHT)

NUMBER OF POINTS: *Pusaq K'uchu Rumi* (Eight Point Stone) aka *Pusaqtin*

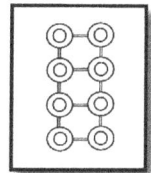

GRAPHICAL REPRESENTATIONS:

GEOMETRIC SHAPE: 8-pointed Star   or Octagon

SYMBOLISM: Infinity

CHAKRA: 8th

COLOR: *Anqas Yuraq* (Blue White)

ANDEAN ARCHETYPE: Llama

ANDEAN TEXTILE DESIGN: *Tawa Inti Qocha* (Four Sun Lake)

APU (Mountain): Wayna Picchu

SAPA INKA: Wiraqocha Inka (Viracocha Inka) Ruled 1410–1438

DIRECTION: *Chanchaysuyu* (Northwest)

CELESTIAL BODY: Pluto

WESTERN ASTROLOGICAL HOUSE: 8 House of Death and Sex

WESTERN ZODIAC ARCHETYPE: Scorpio

CHINESE ZODIAC ARCHETYPE: Sheep

TAROT CARD: Strength / Balance

WESTERN ELEMENT: None

CHINESE ELEMENT: None

TIME OF THE DAY: None

SEASON OF THE YEAR: None

HUMAN ASPECT: None

COMMUNITY CONSCIOUSNESS: None

HUMAN AGE: Afterlife

CYCLE OF LIFE: Decay

PAGAN HOLIDAY (Northern Hemisphere Wheel of the Year): Lughnasadh

PAGAN HOLIDAY (Southern Hemisphere Wheel of the Year): Imbolc

DAY OF THE WEEK: None

MONTH OF THE YEAR: *Awgusto killa* (August)

PERSONALITY: Achievement, Cosmic, Endurance, Karma, Manifestation, Master, Power, Strength

COSMOLOGY:

Eight Universal Andean Spirit Beings: *Mama Unu* (Mother Water); *Mama Allpa* (Mother Earth); *Tayta Inti* (Father Sun); *Tayta Wayra* (Father Wind); *Mama Killa* (Mother Moon); *Mamacha* (Mother Mary); and *Taytacha* (Father Jesus)

NUMBER: ISQUN (NINE)

NUMBER OF POINTS: *Isqun K'uchu Rumi* (Nine Point Stone) aka *Isquntin*

GRAPHICAL REPRESENTATIONS:

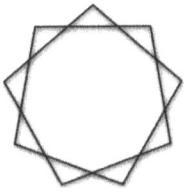

GEOMETRIC SHAPE: 9-pointed Star or Nonagon

SYMBOLISM: Completion

CHAKRA: Right Hand

COLOR: *Qori* (Gold)

ANDEAN ARCHETYPE: Huascar (Last ruler of Inka Empire)

ANDEAN TEXTILE DESIGN: *Inti* (Sun)

APU (Mountain): Pikol

SAPA INKA: Pachakuti Inka Yupanki (Pachacútec) Ruled 1438–1471

DIRECTION: *Ukhupacha* (Below, Lower World)

CELESTIAL BODY: Jupiter

WESTERN ASTROLOGICAL HOUSE: 9 House of Philosophy and Beliefs

WESTERN ZODIAC ARCHETYPE: Sagittarius

CHINESE ZODIAC ARCHETYPE: Monkey

TAROT CARD: Hermit

WESTERN ELEMENT: None

CHINESE ELEMENT: None

TIME OF THE DAY: None

SEASON OF THE YEAR: None

HUMAN ASPECT: None

COMMUNITY CONSCIOUSNESS: None

HUMAN AGE: None

CYCLE OF LIFE: None

PAGAN HOLIDAY (Northern Hemisphere Wheel of the Year): Mabon, Autumn Equinox

PAGAN HOLIDAY (Southern Hemisphere Wheel of the Year): Ostara, Spring Equinox

DAY OF THE WEEK: None

MONTH OF THE YEAR: *Sitimwri killa* (September)

PERSONALITY: Accomplishment, Fulfillment, Humanitarian, Philanthropist, Regeneration

COSMOLOGY:

- Eight Cardinal Directions plus the Center: *Chincha* (North); *Antisuyu* (Northeast); *Intiq Iluqsinan* (East); *Qollasuyu* (Southeast); *Uray* (South); *Kuntisuyu* (Southwest); *Chinchaysuyu* (Northwest); *Intiq Chinkanan* (West); and *Chawpinsuyu* or *Qos'qo* (Center)

- Nine *Qotokuna* (Pleiadian) Stars (Seven Sisters plus Mother and Father): *Puriq qoto* (Asterope/Sterope 1 and 2); *Tarpuq qoto* (Taygeta); *Ñawi qoto* (Maia); *Munay qoto* (Celeano); *Llank'aq qoto* (Electra); *Yllari qoto* (Merope); *K'anchaq qoto* (Alcyone); *Mama qoto* (Pleione); and *Kuraq qoto* (Atlas)

- *Munay Ki* (Energetic Rites of the Four Winds): *Chumpi Mesayoc* (Bands of Power); *Hampe Karpay* (Healer Rite); *Ayni Karpay* (Harmony Rite); *Kawak Karpay* (Seer Rite); *Pampa Mesayoc* (The Daykeeper); *Alto Mesayoc* (The Widsomkeeper); *Kurak Akulleq* (The Earthkeeper); *Mosoq Karpay* (The Starkeeper); and *Tai Tanchis Ranti* (The Creator)

NUMBER: CHUNKA (TEN)

NUMBER OF POINTS: *Chunka K'uchu Rumi* (Ten Point Stone) aka *Chunkantin*

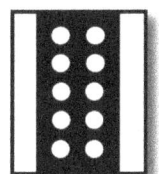

GRAPHICAL REPRESENTATIONS:

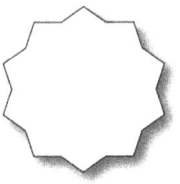   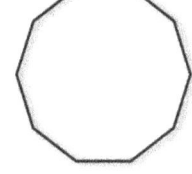

GEOMETRIC SHAPE: 10-pointed Star   or Decagon
SYMBOLISM: Rebirth
CHAKRA: Left Hand
COLOR: *Qolqe* (Silver)
ANDEAN ARCHETYPE: Manco Cápac (Founder of the Cusco and the Inka lineage)
ANDEAN TEXTILE DESIGN: *Ch'ily Qocha* (Body of Water)
APU (Mountain): Pitusiray (Overlooks Chinchero)
SAPA INKA: Tópa Inca (Túpac Inka Yupanqui, Thupa Inka Yupanki) Ruled 1471–1493
DIRECTION: *Hanaqpacha* (Above, Upper World)
WESTERN ASTROLOGICAL HOUSE: 10 House of Social Status and Career
WESTERN ZODIAC ARCHETYPE: Capricorn
CHINESE ZODIAC ARCHETYPE: Rooster
TAROT CARD: Wheel of Fortune / Medicine Wheel
WESTERN ELEMENT: None
CHINESE ELEMENT: None
TIME OF THE DAY: None
SEASON OF THE YEAR: None
HUMAN ASPECT: None

COMMUNITY CONSCIOUSNESS: None

HUMAN AGE: None

CYCLE OF LIFE: None

PAGAN HOLIDAY (Northern Hemisphere Wheel of the Year): None

PAGAN HOLIDAY (Southern Hemisphere Wheel of the Year): None

DAY OF THE WEEK: None

MONTH OF THE YEAR: *Uktuwri killa* (October)

PERSONALITY: Completion, Rebirth, Success, Unification

COSMOLOGY:

Ten Directions: *Chincha* (North); *Antisuyu* (Northeast); *Intiq Iluqsinan* (East); *Qollasuyu* (Southeast); *Uray* (South); *Kuntisuyu* (Southwest); *Intiq Chinkanan* (West); *Chinchaysuyu* (Northwest); *Hanaqpacha* (Above); and *Ukhupacha* (Below)

NUMBER: CHUNKA HUQNIYUQ (ELEVEN)

NUMBER OF POINTS: *Chunka Huqniyuq K'uchu Rumi* (Eleven Point Stone)

GRAPHICAL REPRESENTATIONS:

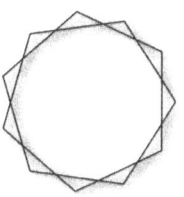

GEOMETRIC SHAPE: 11-pointed Star or Hendecagon

SYMBOLISM: Balance

CHAKRA: Right Foot

COLOR: *Yuraq* (White)

ANDEAN ARCHETYPE: Pachakuti Inka Yupanqui (9th ruler of the Inka Empire, Transformer of the World)

ANDEAN TEXTILE DESIGN: *Pallay* (Pattern Design)

APU (Mountain): Putucus

SAPA INKA: Huayna Cápac (Wayna Qhapaq) Ruled 1493–1527

DIRECTION: *Ukhu* (Within)

WESTERN ASTROLOGICAL HOUSE: 11 House of Community and Friendships

WESTERN ZODIAC ARCHETYPE: Aquarius

CHINESE ZODIAC ARCHETYPE: Dog

TAROT CARD: Justice / Life Force

WESTERN ELEMENT: None

CHINESE ELEMENT: None

TIME OF THE DAY: None

SEASON OF THE YEAR: None

HUMAN ASPECT: None

COMMUNITY CONSCIOUSNESS: None

HUMAN AGE: None

CYCLE OF LIFE: None

PAGAN HOLIDAY (Northern Hemisphere Wheel of the Year): Samhain

PAGAN HOLIDAY (Southern Hemisphere Wheel of the Year): Beltane

DAY OF THE WEEK: None

MONTH OF THE YEAR: *Ayamarq'a Killa* (November)

PERSONALITY: Androgyny, Evolution, Inspiration, Intuition, Master Number, Revelation, Vision

COSMOLOGY

Eleven Directions: *Chincha* (North); *Antisuyu* (Northeast); *Intiq Iluqsinan* (East); *Qollasuyu* (Southeast); *Uray* (South); *Kuntisuyu* (Southwest); *Chinkanan* (West); *Chinchaysuyu* (Northwest); *Intiq* Chawpinsuyu or *Qos'qo* (Center) or *Kaypacha* (Middle); *Hanaqpacha* (Above); and *Ukhupacha* (Below)

NUMBER: CHUNKA ISKAYNIYUQ (TWELVE)

NUMBER OF POINTS: *Chunka Iskayniyuq K'uchu Rumi* (Twelve Point Stone)

GRAPHICAL REPRESENTATIONS: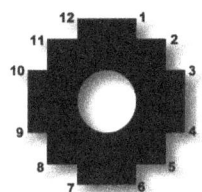

 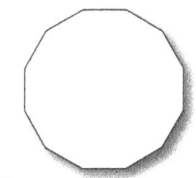

GEOMETRIC SHAPE: 12-Pointed Star or Dodecagon

SYMBOLISM: Mastery

CHAKRA: Left Foot

COLOR: *Puka Llanqa* (Pink)

ANDEAN ARCHETYPE: Wiraqocha, ancient Inka Supreme Deity

ANDEAN TEXTILE DESIGN: *Pallay Tukuy* (Finishing Design)

APU (Mountain): Sawasiray

SAPA INKA: Huascár Inka (Waskhar Inka) Ruled 1527–1532

DIRECTION: *Q'osqo* or Cusco (Center)

WESTERN ASTROLOGICAL HOUSE: 12 House of Spirituality and Self-Undoing

WESTERN ZODIAC ARCHETYPE: Pisces

CHINESE ZODIAC ARCHETYPE: Pig

TAROT CARD: Hanged Man / Vision Quest

WESTERN ELEMENT: None

CHINESE ELEMENT: None

TIME OF THE DAY: None

SEASON OF THE YEAR: None

HUMAN ASPECT: None

COMMUNITY CONSCIOUSNESS: None

HUMAN AGE: None

CYCLE OF LIFE: None

PAGAN HOLIDAY (Northern Hemisphere Wheel of the Year): Yule, Winter Solstice

PAGAN HOLIDAY (Southern Hemisphere Wheel of the Year): Litha, Summer Solstice

DAY OF THE WEEK: None

MONTH OF THE YEAR: *Disimwri killa* (December)

PERSONALITY: Creation, Individualistic, Self-empowerment, Unconventional

COSMOLOGY:

Twelve Inka *Mallku*: 5th level *paq'okuna* (Andean medicine people) will return to Earth during the first stage of the *Taripay Pacha* (the great new age of awareness following the *Pachakuti* or the turning over of time and space). There will be six *Inka Mallku* (male *paq'okuna*) and six *Ñust'a* (female *paq'okuna*). These individuals will have the ability to heal all illnesses with only a touch.

Twelve Inka Months: *Iniru killa* (January), *Hiwriru killa* (February), *Marsu killa* (March), *Awril killa* (April), *Mayu killa* (May), *Huniyu killa* (June), *Huliyu killa* (July), *Awgustu killa* (August), *Sitimwri killa* (September), *Uktuwri killa* (October), *Nuwimbri killa* (November), *Disimbri killa* (December).

Twelve *Ñawi* (Energy Eyes): *Chumpikuna* (Belts) 1 through 5; the right and left eye; the 3rd eye; the right and left hand; and the right and left foot

Twelve Points on the *Chakana* (The Southern Cross star constellation)

Twelve Sacred *Apukuna* (Mountains) in the sacred valley around Cusco: Ausangate, Chimbolla (Illimani), Colquepunku, Huacawilka (also called Huakaywillka, Huacrahuilki 'horn pass', Huacay Huilcay, Waqaywillka, Wayna Willka, Urubamba, and Veronica), Huanacauri, Machu Picchu, Pachatusan, Pikol, Pitusiray, Pumasillo, Salcantay, Sawasiray (Sahuasiyiray), and Viracocahn.

Note: The names of the twelve sacred mountains varies depending on the source of the list. This is because each person in the Andes sources from their own personal connection to the *apukuna* (mountains) and the *chaskakuna* (stars).

Twelve Sapa Inka (excludes Sapa Inka ruling after the Spanish invasion): Manco Cápac, Sinchi Roca, Lloque Yupanqui, Mayta Cápac, Cápac Yupanki, Inka Roca, Yahuár Huacác, Wiraqocha Inka, Pachakuti Inka Yupanki, Tópa Inca, Huayna Cápac, and Huascár Inka

12-sided Stone: A 12-angle stone in the wall of the Palacio del Inca Roca, a 14th-century palace, on Hatun Rumiyoc Street, between Plaza de Armas and San Blas

SUMMARY OF CHUMPI STONE CORRESPONDENCES

	0	1	2	3	4	5	6
Shape	Circle	Dot	Line	Triangle	Square	Pentagon	Hexagon
Symbol	The Unmanifest	Personal Identity	Duality	Movement	Foundation	Orientation	Relationship
Chakra	Earth Star	1st	2nd	3rd	4th	5th	6th
Color	Brown	Red	Orange	Yellow	Green	Blue	Indigo
Andean Archetype	–	Snake or Serpent	Puma or Jaguar	Hummingbird	Condor	Southern Star	Moon
Andean Textile Design	Plain Field	Jungle Dancer	2-Panel Cloth	Mountain	4-Panel Cloth	Southern Star Cloth	Eye
Andean Goddess	–	Mama Ocllo	Mama Mujia	Mama Simona	Doña Theresa	Maria Sakapana	Doña Juana Waman Tiklla
Apu (Mountain)	–	Ausangate	Salkantay	Pachatusan	Huanacauri	Saqsaywaman	Huacawilka
Sapa Inka	–	Manco Cápac	Sinchi Roca	Lloque Yupanqui	Mayta Cápac	Cápac Yupanki	Inka Roca
Direction	–	South	West	North	East	Northeast	Southeast
Celestial Body	Chiron	Mars	Venus	Mercury	Moon	Sun	Juno, Pallas, Vesta
Astrology House	–	1	2	3	4	5	6
Western Zodiac Sign	Ophiuchus	Aries	Taurus	Gemini	Cancer	Leo	Virgo
Chinese Zodiac Sign	–	Rat	Ox	Tiger	Rabbit	Dragon	Snake
Tarot Card	Fool	Magician	High Priestess	Empress	Emperor	Hierophant	Lovers
Western Element	–	Fire	Earth	Air	Water	Ether	–
Chinese Element	–	Fire	Earth	Metal	Water	Wood	–
Kingdom	–	Mineral	Plant	Animal	Human	–	–
Time of Day	–	Sunrise	Noon	Sunset	Midnight	–	–
Season of Year	–	Spring	Summer	Autumn	Winter	–	–
Human Aspect	–	Body	Emotions	Mind	Spirit	–	–
Community Consciousness	–	Family	City	National	Global	Universal	–
Human Age	Conception	Birth	Childhood	Adolescence	Adulthood	Middle Age	Elderhood
Cycle of Life	–	Seed	Germinate	Grow	Bud	Bloom	Mature
Pagan Holiday N Hemi	–	–	Imbolc	Ostara (Spring Equinox)	–	Beltane	Litha (Summer Solstice)
Pagan Holiday S Hemi	–	–	Lughnasadh	Mabon (Autumn Equinox)	–	Samhain	Yule, Inti Raymi (Winter Solstice)
Day of Week	–	Monday	Tuesday	Wednesday	Thursday	Friday	Saturday
Month of Year	–	January	February	March	April	May	June

	7	8	9	10	11	12
Shape	Heptagon	Octagon	Nonagon	Decagon	Hendegagon	Dodecagon
Symbol	Expression	Infinity	Completion	Rebirth	Balance	Mastery
Chakra	7th	8th	Right Hand	Left Hand	Right Foot	Left Foot
Color	Violet	Blue White	Gold	Silver	White	Pink
Andean Archetype	Sun	Llama	Huascár	Manco Capák	Pachakuti	Wiraqocha
Andean Textile Design	Rainbow	4 Sun Lake	Sun	Body of Water	Pattern	Finishing Pattern
Andean Goddess	Doña Tomasa Waman Tiklla	–	–	–	–	–
Apu (Mountain)	Machu Picchu	Wayna Picchu	Pikol	Pitusiray	Putucus	Sawasiray
Sapa Inka	Yahuár Huacác	Wiraqocha Inka	Pachacuti Inka Yupanki	Tópa Inca	Huayna Cápac	Huascár Inka
Direction	Southwest	Northwest	Below	Above	Within	Center
Celestial Body	Ceres	Pluto	Jupiter	Saturn	Uranus	Neptune
Astrology House	7	8	9	10	11	12
Western Zodiac Sign	Libra	Scorpio	Sagittarius	Capricorn	Aquarius	Pisces
Chinese Zodiac Sign	Horse	Sheep	Monkey	Rooster	Dog	Pig
Tarot Card	Chariot	Strength	Hermit	Wheel of Fortune	Justice	Hanged Man
Western Element	–	–	–	–	–	–
Chinese Element	–	–	–	–	–	–
Kingdom	–	–	–	–	–	–
Time of Day	–	–	–	–	–	–
Season of Year	–	–	–	–	–	–
Human Aspect	–	–	–	–	–	–
Community Consciousness	–	–	–	–	–	–
Human Age	Death	Afterlife	–	–	–	–
Cycle Of Life	Wilt	Decay	–	–	–	–
Pagan Holiday N Hemi	–	Lughnasadh	Mabon (Autumn Equinox)	–	Samhain	Yule (Winter Solstice)
Pagan Holiday S Hemi	–	Imbolc	Ostara (Spring Equinox)	–	Beltane	Litha (Summer Solstice)
Day of Week	Sunday	–	–	–	–	–
Month of Year	July	August	September	October	November	December

CHAPTER 4

OTHER CARVED COMPANIONS

TAWAY (Dice)

An Andean *taway* has images instead of dots that represent numbers. The images identify the energetics of what is to come when used in divination. Below is a chart showing the most common images found on these dice. When I find dice in the markets of Pisac, Peru, I ask the vendor what meaning is attached to the images. There does not seem to be a universal meaning for the images so I suspect that the stewards of the dice attach their personal meaning to them. I would suggest this practice for you when you obtain your own set.

DICE IMAGE	IMAGE INTERPRETATION	WESTERN INTERPRETATION	ANDEAN REPRESENTATION
	Wayra	Wind	Travel or Work without Hindrance
	Chacra	Fields	Blessings for the Home or Good Health
	Inti	Sun	Energy or Good Day
	Chaska	Star	Work or Love to the Dearest Beings
	Killa	Moon	Money or Good Night
	Kuka	Coca	Love or Prevention for Good Health
	Qhapaqñan	Energy Pathway	Unknown

Dice can be used for divination by first setting your request or question. Then roll the die. Lastly, interpret the results based on what image is shown on top. If you use more than one die, also note their physical relationship to one another.

Dice can also be used as game pieces. Create your own game and then share it with other members of your *ayllu* (community).

TIHA RUMI (Tile Stone)

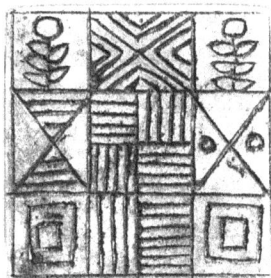 

Tiha are *huamanga* (alabaster) tiles that bring together sacred symbols of the Andean tradition. The tile stone pictured on the left is a calendar. I have not found any source that can identify how it works. However, the images look familiar. (To interpret them, please refer to the image directory in the next chapter.)

There is also a style of *tiha* that is used to teach about different relationships in Andean cosmology. There are four basic types of energetic arrangements:

AYNI – A reciprocity or mutual exchange that establishes right relationship. The purpose of practicing *ayni* it to create balance and harmony. It is the core guiding principle of the Andean people. Anything or anyone that is in right relationship with another is called *hapu ranti*.

YANANTIN – The joining together of two dissimilar energies in a harmonious relationship is *yanantin*. For example: dry and wet; cold and warm; sun and moon; right and left; day and night; masculine and feminine; birth and death. The harmonious integration of two dissimilar energies is called *hapu*.

MASINTIN – The joining together of two similar energies in a harmonious relationship. For example: two men (both masculine); two women (both feminine); planets and stars (all celestial); mountains and valleys (all terrestrial). The harmonious integration of two similar energies is called *ranti*.

TAWANTIN – The joining together of four energies in a harmonious relationship.

Note: Any two energies that are in relationship form a third powerful and unique energy.

Below is a *hapu ranti tiha* that shows *yanantin* and *masintin* energy relationships.

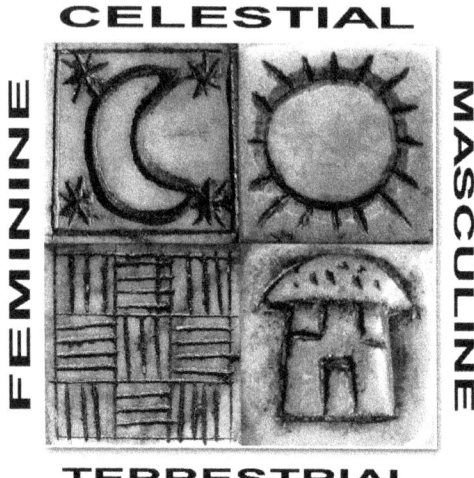

One can identify the following relationships on it:

- *Hapu: Inti* (sun) energy is *yanantin* to *Killa* (moon) energy
- *Hapu: Wasi* (house, contained by a structure) energy is *yanantin* to *Chacra* (field, open, expansive, outside a structure) energy
- *Ranti:* The Celestial energies of *Inti* and *Killa* are *masintin*
- *Ranti:* The Terrestrial energies of *Chacra* and *Wasi* are *masintin*
- *Ranti:* The Feminine energies of *Killa* and *Chacra* are *masintin*
- *Ranti:* The Masculine energies of *Inti* and *Wasi* are *masintin*
- *Hapu Ranti:* The Celestial energy is in *ayni* with the Terrestrial energy
- *Hapu Ranti:* The Masculine energy is in *ayni* with the Feminine energy
- *Inti, Killa, Chacra,* and *Wasi* are *Tawantin* on this tile stone

MAKIKUNA (Hands)

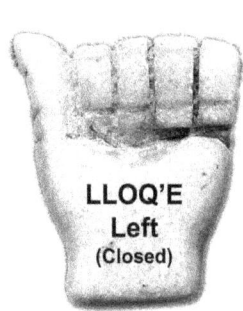 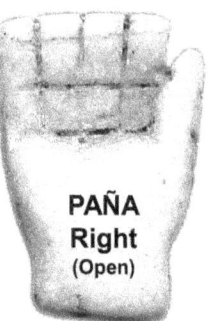 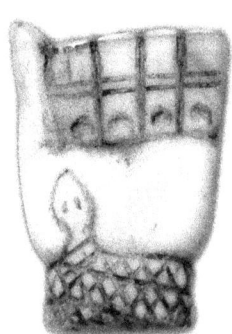 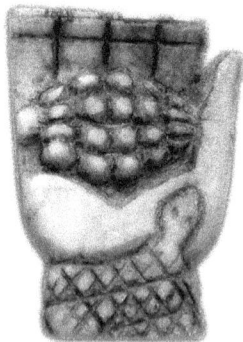

Huamanga (alabaster) hands are often found in the marketplaces. Some of the hands have images carved on them, as shown on the right, and some do not, as shown on the left. Some *makikuna* are carved in *hiwaya* (meteorite stone). The hands are used in energy work. There is different meaning attached to the right and left:

LLOQ'E MAKI (Left Hand) — The left hand is the Hand of Receptivity and is used to receive or hold energy. It represents: our inner world, the magical world, the sacred/spiritual world, the lunar world, the Feminine, and holding energy.

PAÑA MAKI (Right Hand) – The right hand is the Hand of Power and is used to extend or project energy. It represents: our outer world, the mystical world, the secular world, the solar world, the Masculine, and projecting energy.

CONOPAKUNA (Votive Offerings)

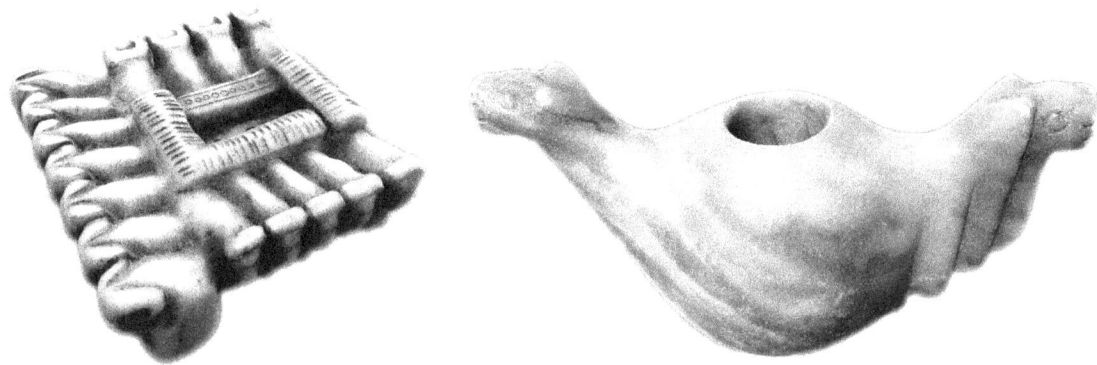

The *conopa*, *canopa*, or *qonopa* is an essential piece of the Andean family altar. They are used as a way to petition for the fertility of their animals and crops. They can also be used to manifest other desires such as protection, luck, prosperity, success, and good health. *Canopakuna* are placed in the home and in the corrals. They are most commonly carved from *huamanga* (alabaster) or wood. The typical form is that of llamas, alpaca, or sheep. The *canopa* serves as an offering vessel. In ceremony, llama or alpaca fat or coca leaves are placed within the center receptacle.

CHAPTER 5

VISUAL DIRECTORY OF CARVED IMAGES

IMAGES ARE MYTHIC STORIES

Just as the symbols woven into Andean textiles are representations of energy, so are the symbols that are carved into objects. Images are primal because there is no need for language to understand them. Pictures are their own language. They hold at least three layers of meaning: the association that the artist has, the association that the viewer draws from their own personal experience, and the mythic meaning that is held in the collective consciousness. Images are powerful because they bypass the logical mind and access the sensory perceptions of the viewer. Images are the unspoken language of ancient peoples as well as the energetic language many Spirit Beings use.

The style of the carved images varies from artist to artist. The owners of the carved objects may even add their own symbols to the objects. If you obtain a set of *chumpi* stones previously owned by an Andean *paq'o* (medicine person), they may have personal symbols etched into them.

> "All symbols, whether sacred or quite ordinary, are a bridge between the seen and the unseen. Symbols are intended to make things that are intangible or too vast to comprehend into something that fits into human experience."
>
> –Eleanora Amendolara, author of *Chumpi Illumination: Gateways to Healing and Transformation*

I am not aware of any written documentation on the interpretation of carved images from the Andes. The interpretations of the carved images shown below have been given to me through word of mouth from various sources in the Andes. I find it fascinating to see how different artisans present the images. There is no set rule or tradition, however, through my work with these symbols, I have noticed a group of images that appear more frequently on *chumpi* stone sets. They are:

Chapter 5: Visual Directory of Carved Images 71

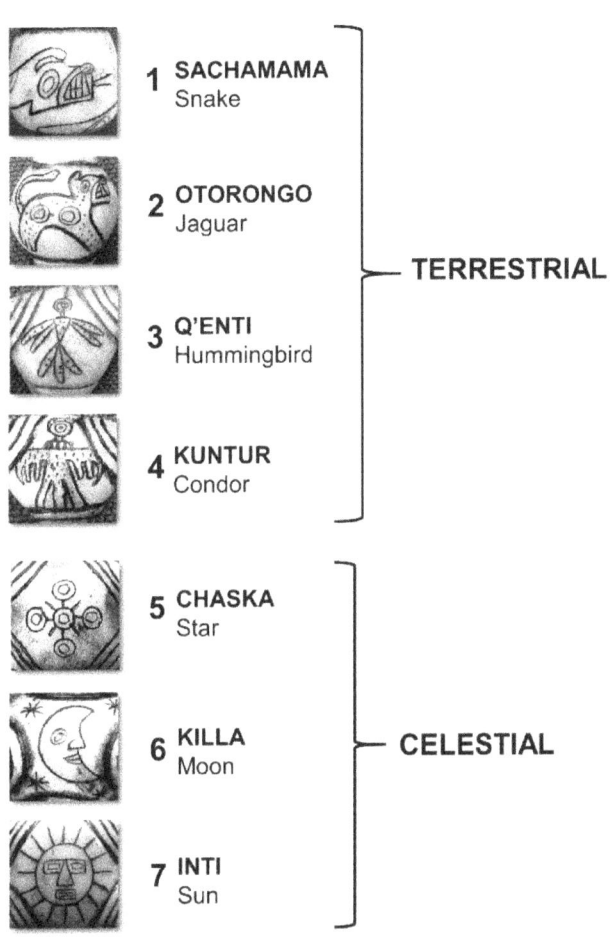

The same holds true for *taway* (dice). The images carved on each *taway* differ from artist to artist. There is no set rule or tradition, however, I have noticed the following group of images that appear most frequently on *taway*:

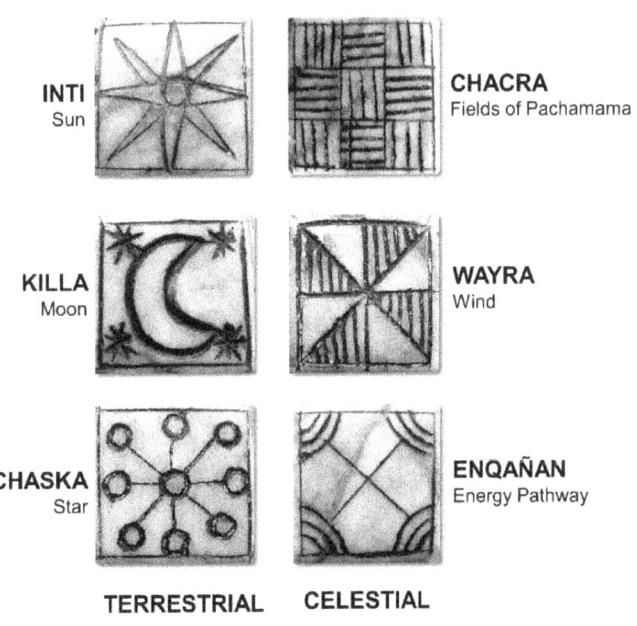

DIRECTORY OF IMAGES

The images carved on *chumpi* stones and dice are shown in the next section in alphabetical order. All of the items shown in this book are in the private collections of myself or Robert Wakeley Wheeler. I have listed the basic or simplest interpretation of the images as I have gathered from Andean artisans and medicine people. Any image can have multiple interpretations based on cultural and personal experiences. As in all things, honor your own perspective based on your knowledge, intuition, and experiences.

Note: I welcome learning about any images that you have found that are not included in this chapter.

CHACRA or **PAMPA** – Field. The Great Mother, fertility, the terrestrial, provider, nourisher.

CHAKANA – The Southern Cross star constellation. Guidance, the Tree of Life, the symbology of four.

CHASKA or **CHASKA WARANI** – Star or Constellation. Guidance, the celestial, eternity, agent of divination.

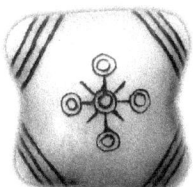 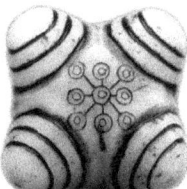 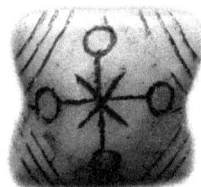 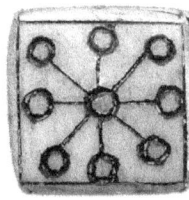 

CHULPA aka **QOLLQA** – Storage Structure (Some other interpretations have been Snail or Lagoon with Fish). Storage is holding, a snail is slowness and rebirth, the lagoon is feminine emotion.

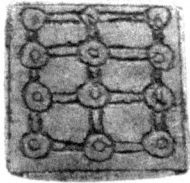

CH'UNCHU – Jungle Dancer. The indigenous soul, origins, wild Nature.

ILLAPA – Lightning. Enlightenment, illumination, Divine Power.

INTI aka **INTI TAYTA** – Sun aka Father Sun. Supreme Cosmic Power, the Universal Father (in most traditions), creative energy.

KILLA aka **MAMA KILLA** – Moon aka Mother Moon. Cyclic time, The Universal Mother (in most traditions), intuition.

K'INTU – Coca Prayer Leaves (usually in a group of three). Prayer breath, integration of body, mind, and heart, representation of the three shamanic worlds (*Ukhupacha*: Lower World; *Kaypacha*: Middle World); *Hanaqpacha*: Upper World), representation of the three human attributes (*llank'ay*: action, *munay*: love, and *yachay*: wisdom), representation of the three primary energies (*kawsay*: life force energy, *sami*: high vibratory energy, and *k'anchay*: light energy).

KUKA – Coca Plant. Energizer, stimulation, sustenance,

KUNTUR – Condor. All-seeing, ascension, release from bondage, sky gods.

  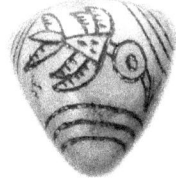  

KUTIY or **KUTY** – Infinity. Immortality, perpetuity.

MAKI – Hand. Power, action, transmitter of energy.

MUYUMA – Spiral. Life force, vortex, emanation. A spiral is bi-directional: energy moves from the core to the outer world and from the other world to the core.

PARA, RIT'I, and CHIKCHI – Rain, Snow, and Hail aka Precipitation. Fecundity, fertilizer, purification, source of life.

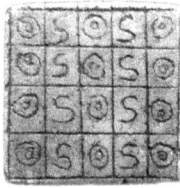

PHAQCHA – Waterfall. Cleansing, purity, source of life, spiritual nourishment.

PUMA or **OTORONGO** or **CHINCHAY** – Cougar or Jaguar. (Refer to notes on *Otorongo* in the glossary.) Messenger of the forest spirits, a powerful protector, an eater of *hucha* (heavy energy).

Q'ENTI – Hummingbird. Lightness of being, swiftness, endurance, enjoyment of life, a bringer of *sami* (high vibratory energy).

QHAPAQÑAN – Energy Pathway; Inka Road to the *Tawantinsuyu* (Four Regions of the Inka Empire). Movement, purpose, direction, choice.

SACH'AMAMA or **AMARU** – Serpent or Snake. Renewal, sexuality, fertility, procreative masculine power, the complementary pairs of solar and lunar, life and death, light and darkness, good and evil, healing and poinson, preservation and destruction.

  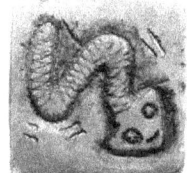

SARA aka **MAMA SARA** – Corn aka Mother Corn. Earth's fertility, sustenance, abundance.

 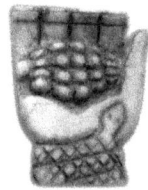

TAWANTINSUYU – Four Regions of the Inka Empire. Spatial order of the universe, organization, stability, foundation.

T'IKA – Flower (The last example could also be interpreted as snow.) Feminine reception, innocence, beauty, brevity of life, youth.

WASI – House. Shelter, protection, our Cosmic Center.

WAYRA – Wind or air. Spirit, messenger of the gods, animation, breath.

THE 3 SHAMANIC WORLDS – *Ukhupacha* (Lower World); *Kaypacha* (Middle World); *Hanaqpacha* (Upper World). This is also interpreted as crops, such as maize (corn) and quinoa. The symbolism of crops is Earth's fertility, sustenance, abundance.

CHAPTER 6

CHUMPI STONE USES

A BIRTHING RITUAL FOR CHUMPI STONES

Rituals are a set of symbolic actions that are performed to activate intention, create focus, and move energy. Rituals elevate the mundane, secular, and ordinary to the special, sacred, and extraordinary. Rituals connect our earthbound soul to the spirit world. Our guides and ancestors consider them an invitation to join us. At a minimum, you will want to create a "birthing" ritual to welcome a new set of *chumpi* stones into your collection of sacred tools. You can create your own ritual or follow the welcoming ritual given below.

1. Design your ritual. What is your goal? Where will you do it? Who will participate? When will you do it? What tools and supplies do you want to use, such as candles, clothing, drink, food, flowers, incense, etc.

2. Gather your tools and prepare your area as well as yourself. Wash your hands in cool running water both before and after the ritual. Wear some special clothing to separate your spiritual self from your secular self.

3. Create a safe and sacred space in which to work in the usual way that you do by establishing protection and purifying your space. Invite your spirit guides and ancestors. You may want to build a sacred fire outside or light some candles inside.

4. Establish your intent by reciting a prayer, affirmation, or blessing you have prepared either silently or out loud. In this case, be sure to ask for your *chumpi* stones to be blessed as you welcome them into your home.

5. Perform a cleansing of your *chumpi* stones by choosing methods from the list below. Keep your intention in mind as you clear away all inappropriate energies. Visualize the *chumpi* stones as sparkly, tingly, cool, alive, and working with you.

6. Sit with your *chumpi* stones for a time, then ask them for any messages they have brought to you now. You may want to record these messages in your journal.

7. Make an offering of *ayni* (reciprocity) and gratitude by giving something to Mother Earth. This can be cornmeal, flowers, libations, tobacco, a piece of your hair, or any other materials that have significance to you. You may want to also offer chants, bell-ringing, dancing, songs, or music from flutes and drums.

8. Release your sacred space when the ritual is complete. Thank all spirits who have participated.

CLEANSING CHUMPI STONES

When you obtain your *chumpi* stones you will want to cleanse and energize them (as you would for all of your sacred tools). Then repeat this process periodically. Some people believe that *chumpi* stones are self-cleansing and therefore do not need to be cleansed. It is up to you to decide what is appropriate for your own stones.

Cleansing is both a physical process and a spiritual ritual. Since *chumpi* stones become receptive to emotional energies, cleansing will neutralize them. A cleared *chumpi* stone feels bright, tingly, and cool to the touch. A *chumpi* stone that needs clearing may feel hot, heavy, drained, or life-less. Below are some suggestions of how to cleanse your *chumpi* stones.

Note: Although water is usually an excellent purifier, do not cleanse your *chumpi* stones and other *khuya* (sacred stones) in water as this may deteriorate the characteristics of the stone as well as erase its energetic information.

SUNLIGHT AND MOONLIGHT – Energize your *chumpi* stones in sunlight and moonlight for 24 hours. Your *chumpi* stones need a day of sunlight and a night of moonlight to re-energize. The time of the full moon is perfect for this. (*Note:* Do not put amethyst in sunlight.)

CANDLE LIGHT – Place a candle in a safe space. You may also write your intention on a piece a paper and place it under the candle. Light the candle, then pass each *chumpi* stone back and forth just above the flame several times. You may want to leave your stones in a circle surrounding the candle for a period of time, however, make sure your candle is attended at all times for safety reasons.

SMUDGING – Smudge your *chumpi* stones by burning a wedge of dried herbs such as sage, sandalwood, cedar, mugwort, or sweet grass. Wave the smoke over the stones or pass the stones through the smoke. Many individuals may want to use Palo Santo, however, it may be endangered from over-harvesting. Always obtain your Palo Santo and herbs from quality suppliers who only support sustainable harvesters.

SMOKELESS SMUDGING – Blow Florida water over your *chumpi* stones. Florida water, when combined with the prayer of your breath, is a very powerful cleansing technique used extensively in the Andes.

PRAYER BREATH – Hold each *chumpi* stone, one at a time, in front of your mouth. Blow across the stone. You may also hold a bit of Florida water in your mouth and blow it across the stone. This not only cleanses the stone but also blesses the stone with your prayer. In Peru, this process is called *phukuy* (prayerful breath by blowing). You can create your own essences for spiritual spraying as an alternative to commercial Florida water. I personally use a vodka base with various essential oils added to it.

SEA SALT – Place dry sea salt in a glass and bury the stones in the salt. Leave overnight. Be sure to use sea salt only, table salt contains iodine, aluminum and other unwanted chemicals.

HERBS – Bury your *chumpi* stones in a cupful of dried herbs such as rose petals, sage, clover, daisies, comfrey, or sandalwood. This is a gentle way to clear stones but it does require longer than leaving the stones overnight in sea salt.

EARTH BURIAL – Bury the *chumpi* stones under the earth for 24 hours. Earth consists of very powerful magnetic energy fields that will cleanse your stones of all negativity effectively. Apartment dwellers can use a flower pot full of soil.

RESONATING SOUND – Purify your *chumpi* stones with the resonating sound of a bell, Tibetan singing bowl, tuning fork, or anything that creates a pure sound such as the OM mantra. Hold your stones close to the origin of the sound for a few minutes.

CRYSTAL PENDULUM – Pass a clear crystal pendulum in a counterclockwise circle over the *chumpi* stones nine times. Then reverse the pendulum and circle it slowly in a clockwise direction nine times.

AMETHYST OR QUARTZ BED – Leave your *chumpi* stones on an amethyst bed for 24 hours or place your *chumpi* stones on a large cleansed quartz crystal cluster for a few hours. Amethyst transmutes lower energies into the higher frequencies. The very strong crystalline energies present within the quartz will neutralize any negative energies to be found within your *chumpi* stones.

VISUALIZATION – Hold your *chumpi* stones in your hand and say these words, "*I command that these chumpi stones be self-cleansing*" or "*I invoke the Light of Love and Spirit to cleanse these chumpi stones*". As you repeat these words you should visualize the negative energies falling away from your stone and only the natural and pure energies remaining.

ENERGIZING CHUMPI STONES

Once your *chumpi* stones are cleansed, you may want to energize them. Here are some suggested ways:

REIKI ENERGY – Infuse Reiki energy (if you are an attuned Reiki practitioner) into your *chumpi* stones as a way to prepare them for use.

ANOINT WITH ESSENTIAL OILS – Anoint your *chumpi* stones (if the type of material is safe for this technique) with an essential oil or intention oil. Frankincense is often used for spiritual purposes. However, sources say that frankincense trees are endangered from over-tapping. Always obtain your frankincense from quality suppliers who only support sustainable harvesters. You can also use alternatives such as cypress, juniper, sandalwood, myrrh, or lavender.

CALL TO SPIRIT GUIDES AND POWER ANIMALS – Petition your spirit guides or power animals to provide protection for your *chumpi* stones.

MEDITATION AND JOURNEYING – Meditate or journey to the *chumpi* stones to ask for specific messages related to the stones' purposes, uses, care, and relationship to yourself.

AFFIRMATION WORK

If you would like to perform affirmation work, place crystal *chumpi* stone sets into grid patterns. The energetic field expands exponentially when grids are activated. The geometric pattern of the grid directs energy toward a goal set by your intention. Crystals have a natural capacity to amplify energy. Information can be stored in the molecular structure of a quartz crystal. Crystals also have the ability to transmute energy from one form, such as *hucha* (dense energy) into another form, such as *sami* (high vibratory energy).

Crystal grids can be used for:

- Protection from psychic attack
- Grounding
- Manifesting desires
- Spiritual and physical body healing work
- Long distance healing
- Charging objects with life-force energy

There are many books about building crystal grids and many grids that can be built from the simple to the very complex. I like to use a very simple 4-sided grid that utilizes five *chumpi* stones plus one *chumpi* or a crystal to use as a pointer. A clear quartz single terminated crystal makes a great pointer.

The 4-sided grid pattern fits very nicely with the *tawantin* (relationship of four) in Andean cosmology, so I call it *"The Tawantin"*. It can be used to align with the four bodies (physical, emotional, mental, spiritual), the four directions (north, east, south, west), and the four elements (earth, water, fire, and air). The grid pattern is adapted from some of the teachings of my crystal grid teacher, Dael Walker, author of *The Crystal Book* and *The Crystal Healing Book*.

Steps to Building and Activating a *Chumpi* Stone Grid

1. **Determine the intention of the grid.** The most important action when making affirmation grids is that your intention be clear. Always state a specific intention in a clear and concise statement. Make only one intention per grid rather than compound requests. Be ethical by only making affirmations for yourself or what you have stewardship over unless you have obtained informed consent to act for another person. You may want to write down your intention on a paper and place it at the base of your grid to amplify its message.

2. **Select a *chumpi* stone set.** Refer to the material properties of crystals to determine those best suited to support your intention. (Refer to page 12) Clear quartz is a universal crystal that has a neutral energy frequency that can be programmed with any intent. It is a powerful amplifier of energy.

3. **Select a base for your grid.** An Andean textile with woven symbols is ideal. Refer to the symbolic properties of textile symbols to choose one best suited to support your intention. (Refer to page 25) If you do not have any Andean textiles, you can scan, then print out, symbols from this book and use them as a base for your grid.

4. **Clear the *chumpi* stones, cloth, and the area that you will be working in.** (For cleansing techniques, refer to page 78) Open sacred space as you usually do for sacred work.

5. **Place the *chumpi* stones on the base you have chosen to work with.** You can use the diagrams below to set up the stones. Templates are also available on the website at www.ChumpiSacredStones.com. The grid should be set up in a place where it will not be disturbed. If any item in the grid is moved, the activation of the grid will be cancelled.

6. **Pick up the item you have chosen as the pointer.** Point it at the center stone and say the following invocation out loud 3 times: "*I invoke the Light of Spirit within. I am a clear and perfect channel. Light and Love is my Guide.*"

7. **Activate the grid.** Using the pointer, move from the center stone to the outer stones in the pattern shown on the template. Repeat your intention out loud as you move from stone to stone to activate the grid. When stating your intention, you might consider adding this phrase at the end: "*…for my highest good, for my optimum health, with grace and ease*".

Clockwise Tawantin (4-sided) Grid for Healing Petitions

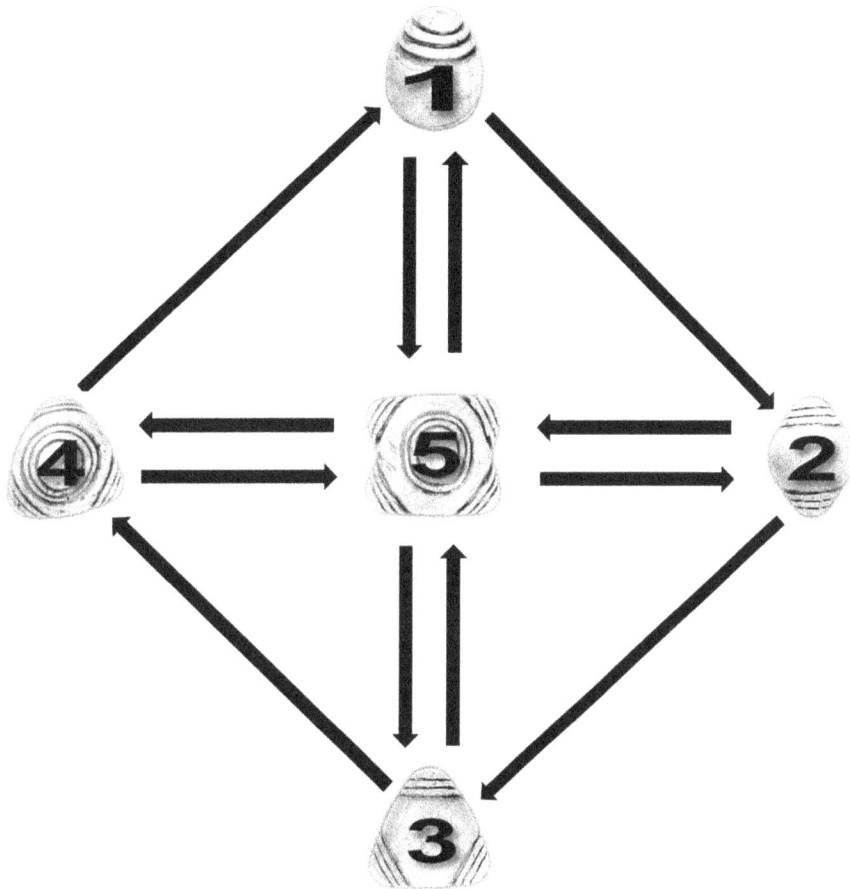

Activate the grid clockwise to focus the energy into the earth. All petitions for healing, grounding, or protection go clockwise since the human body is of and from the earth. It does not matter which stone is activated first as long as you follow the clockwise pattern.

Counterclockwise Tawantin (4-sided) Grid for All Other Petitions

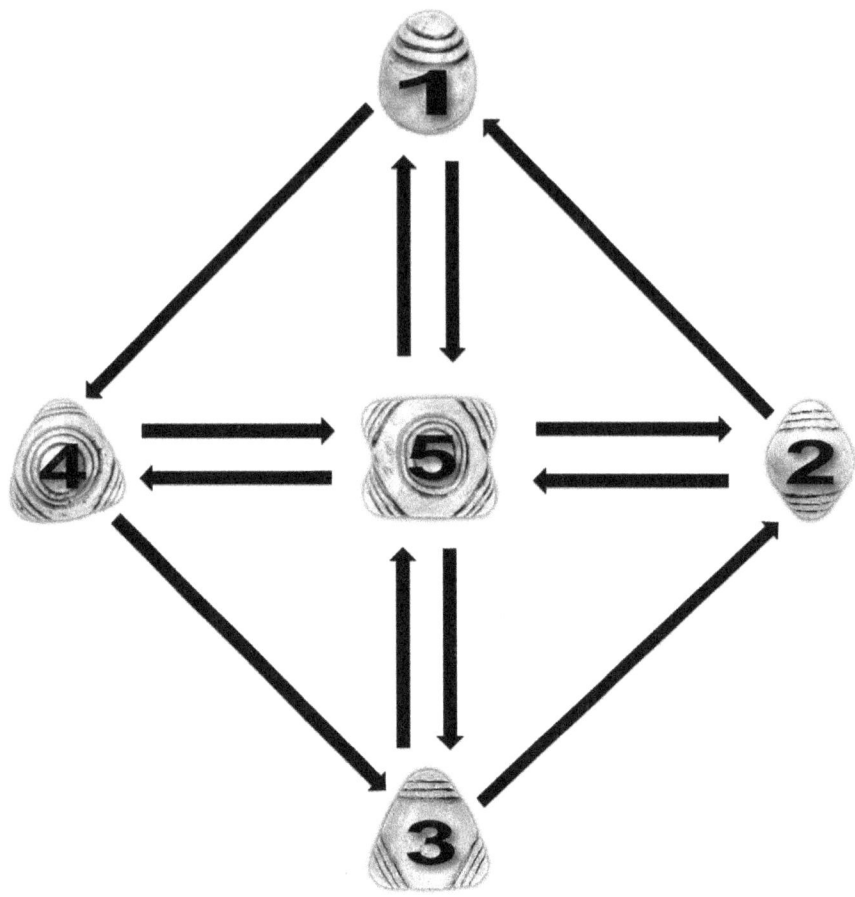

Activate the grid counterclockwise to focus the energy into the universe. All other petitions should go counterclockwise so energy moves into the Universe to be fulfilled. It does not matter which stone is activated first as long as you follow the counterclockwise pattern.

8. **You can repeat the programming as often as you wish.** Perhaps you might want to do it daily for number of days. This will reinforce your affirmation.

9. **Cancelling the grid.** Move any item from the grid pattern when you feel your intention has manifested, the energy of the grid has depleted, or the time the grid is active is complete. This will cancel the activation of the intention. Cleanse your materials before reusing.

DIVINATION WORK

1. Use a *Huq* (Number 1) *chumpi* stone as a pointer. Place it on one of the grids below. Templates of these grids are available at the website www.ChumpiSacredStones.com.

2. Create your question by asking specific, simple, clear, and concise wording. Ask only one question at a time. Do not ask compound questions using "and" or "or." Only ask questions about yourself or what you have stewardship over unless you have obtained informed consent to do divination for another person.

3. Spin the *chumpi* pointer while focusing on your question.

Condition Grid

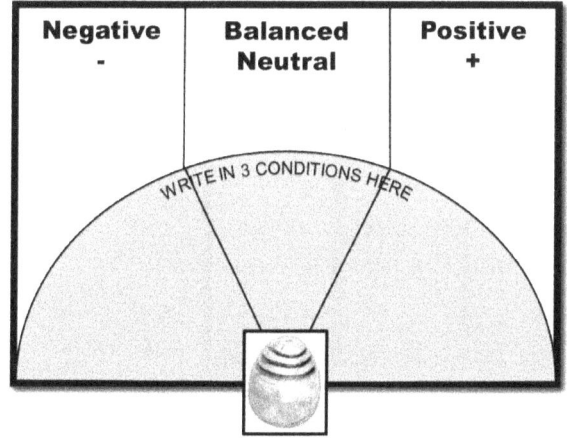

Yes–No Grid #1

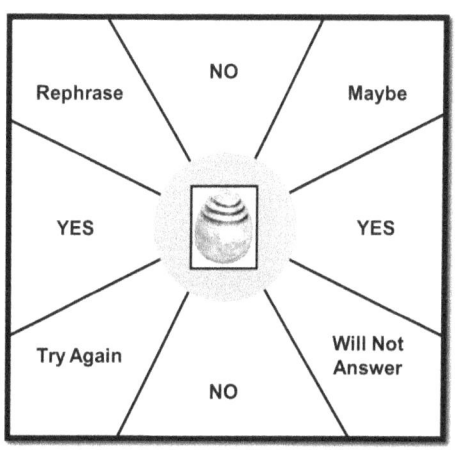

Yes–No Grid #2

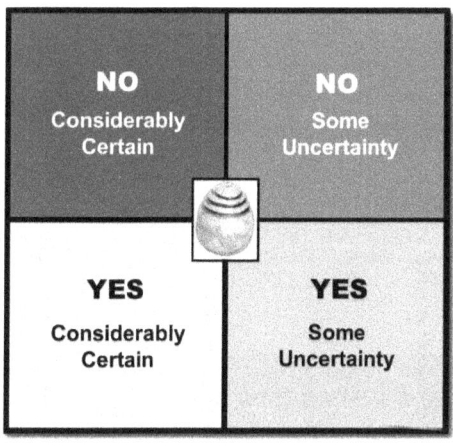

Time–Space Grid

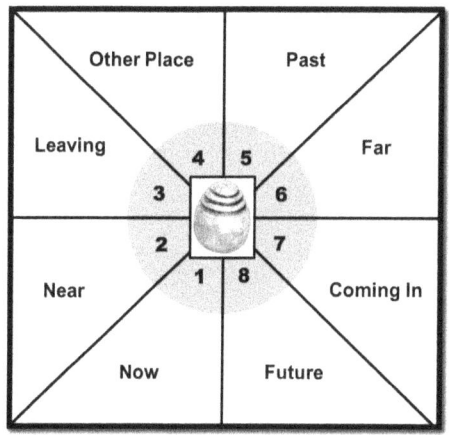

You might also tie a *chumpi* stone to a string, cord, or rope to create a pendulum. A #5 *chumpi* with the *chaska* (star) symbol would work especially well as it represents a navigation device. Templates of pendulum grids are available at the website www.ChumpiSacredStones.com.

Yes–No Grid #1

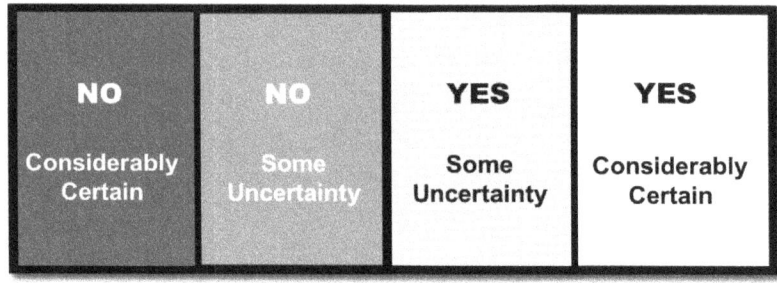

Yes–No Grid #2

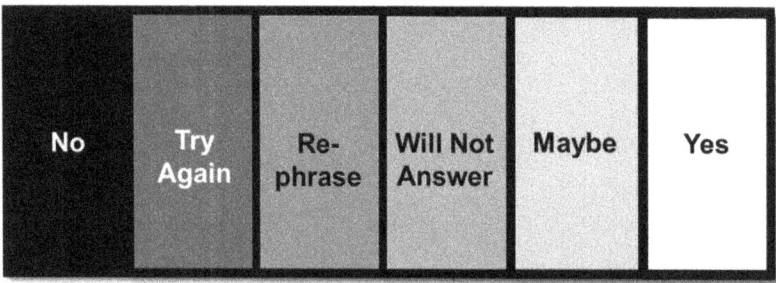

Quantitative Questions

Space-Time Questions

CHAPTER 7

ENERGY WORK WITH CHUMPI STONES

THE ENERGY BODY

The spiritual and healing practices of the Andean medicine people are based on the principles of the energy body. Therefore, if you wish to use *chumpi* stones for these purposes, you will want to have a good understanding of human energetics. In this chapter, I present a concise overview of human energy systems. If this is your first introduction to the energy body, I encourage you to continue researching other sources such as the internet and books. I personally find this subject to be fascinating.

The Physical Body, the form we are most familiar with, is the container that holds a soul while it is incarnated in the 3rd dimension (i.e. on Earth). The Physical Body consists of energy so dense that it can be felt and seen. There is an additional form of the soul which consists of energetic layers surrounding the physical body, that is less dense energy and thus not visible to most people. The Energy Body is known by various names in different spiritual, esoteric, occult, and mystical teachings:

- Poq'po (Andean tradition)
- Light Body, Rainbow Body, or Shining Body (Tibetan Buddhist tradition)
- Subtle Body (Yoga tradition)
- Body of Bliss (Kriya Yoga tradition)
- Diamond Body (Taoist tradition)
- Divine Body (Tantric tradition)
- Superconductive Body (Vedanta tradition)
- Sacred Body and Supra-celestial Body (Sufi tradition)
- Immortal Body (Hermetic tradition)
- Golden Body (Alchemical tradition)
- Perfect Body (Mithraic tradition)
- Radiant Body (Gnostic tradition)
- Resurrection Body or Glorified Body (Christian tradition)
- Luminous Body or Being (*akh*) or Karast (Ancient Egyptian tradition)
- Luminous Energy Field (LEF) (The Four Winds Shamanic School)
- Aura (Psychic traditions)

Our Energy Body is a luminous body that can travel in other dimensions. The Energy Body system includes the following components: *kawsay, ch'i, ki,* or *prana* (living energy); *chakras* or *ñawikuna* (energy vortexes); *nadis, ceques,* or meridians (energy channels); and *poq'po,* aura, or subtle body (energy bubbles).

The Energy Body can be differentiated into multiple layers. The number and names of the layers vary according to different spiritual models and theories. Some of these layers are close to the Physical Body, while the outer layers extend into other dimensions of the spirit world. At least one of those layers, called the "Higher Self", never descends to the physical body, but remains resident on the spiritual planes. The Higher Self retains all of a soul's consciousness and memories and plays the role of overseer of all of the soul's energetic piece parts.

The following diagram is a simplified depiction of the Energy Body layers.

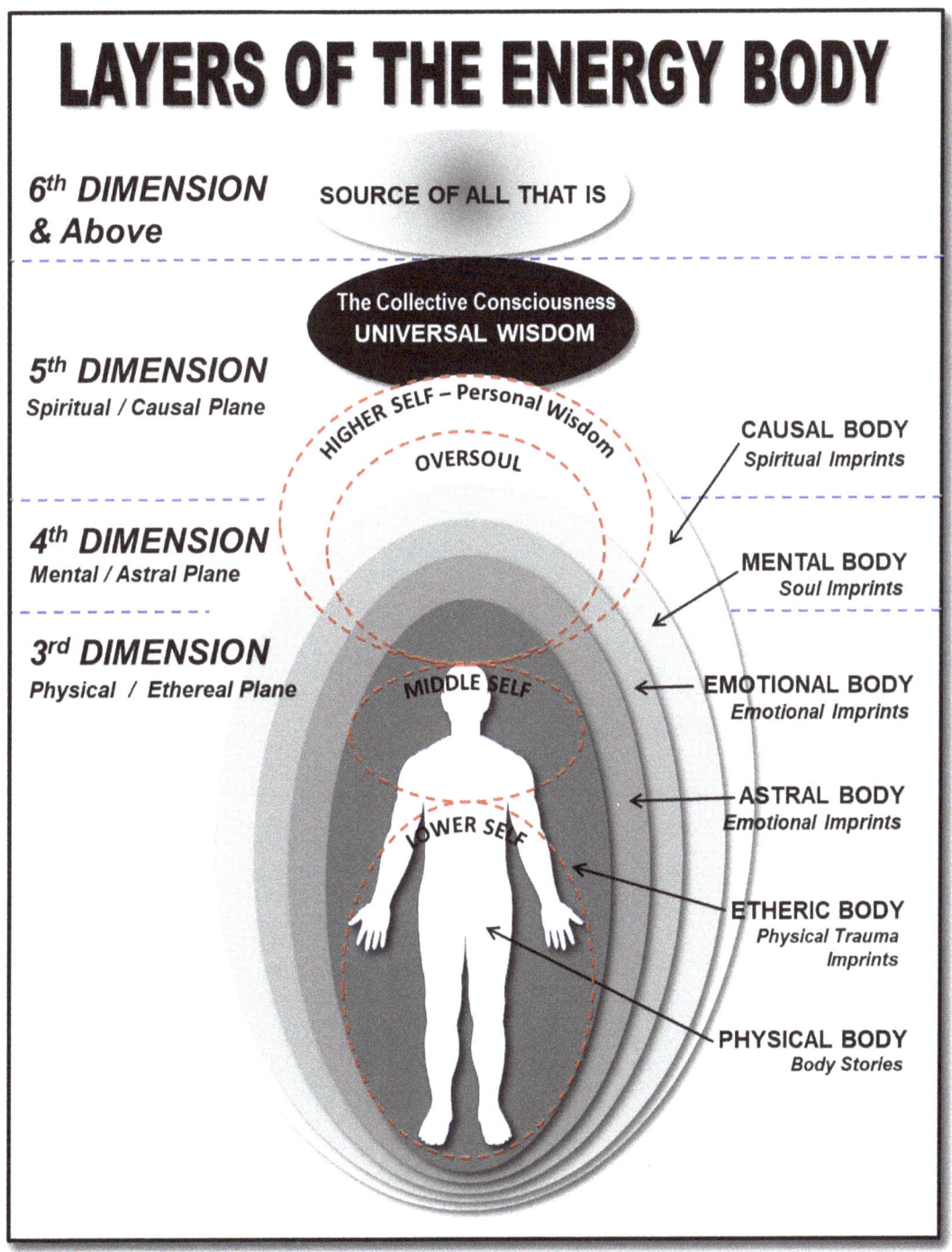

The following chart lists the differences between the Energy Body and the Physical Body:

ENERGY BODY (EB)	PHYSICAL BODY (PB)
Is Formless.	Has Form.
Exists in Timelessness.	Exists in Linear Time.
Composed of energy as Light.	Composed of energy as Dense Matter.
Maintains a connected Oneness identity.	Maintains a separate Ego identity.
A product of past lives and karmic activity.	A product of ancestors and genetic material.
Memories are stored in the Akashic records.	Memories are stored in the genes and passed through heredity.
Has high energy, low density.	Has low energy, high density.
Stores trauma from past lifetimes.	Stores trauma from the current incarnation.
Does not age and does not die.	Ages and dies.
Is immortal and is kept over many lifetimes.	Is mortal and kept only for the current incarnation.
Taken with you when you die.	Left on Earth when you die.
Can be seen by the mind's (third) eye. Can be seen by the physical eye but more often is felt.	Can be seen by the physical eye and experienced through the other four senses.
Eternal. Is carried in between lives and through multiple lives.	Temporary. Only lasts one lifetime.
Exists on the higher planes of existence (i.e. the spiritual world).	Exists on the Physical Plane (i.e. the third dimension).
Shamanic & Energy Medicine Practitioners work on the EB.	Western Medicine works on the PB. Eastern Medicine works on both EB & PB.

THE ANDEAN ENERGY SYSTEM

Much of the knowledge of the Andean energy body has come to the West through Juan Nuñez del Prado, an Andean priest, anthropologist, and keeper of the Q'ero traditions.

To learn more about Andean energy body work, Joan Parisi Wilcox's book, *Masters of the Living Energy: The Mystical World of the Q'ero of Peru* or Elizabeth B. Jenkins's book, *The Fourth Level: Nature Wisdom Teachings of the Inka* are both excellent sources.

The Andean *ñawi* (eyes) are similar to the Hindu *chakras*. There are eyes in each of the five *chumpikuna* (bands or belts). The top four eyes point to the front of the body and the bottom eye points to the back of the body. There are also *ñawikuna* at the top of the head, in the palms of the hands, and on the soles of the feet. The *qos'qo* is similar to the Asian concept of the *hara*. It is the energy center that resides in the belly. *Paq'okuna* (Andean medicine people) learn how to feel, eat, and digest energy through the *qos'qo*. The *poq'po* is the energy body or bubble of energy surrounding the physical body.

Below is a diagram that shows the Andean energy systems of the body from the side.

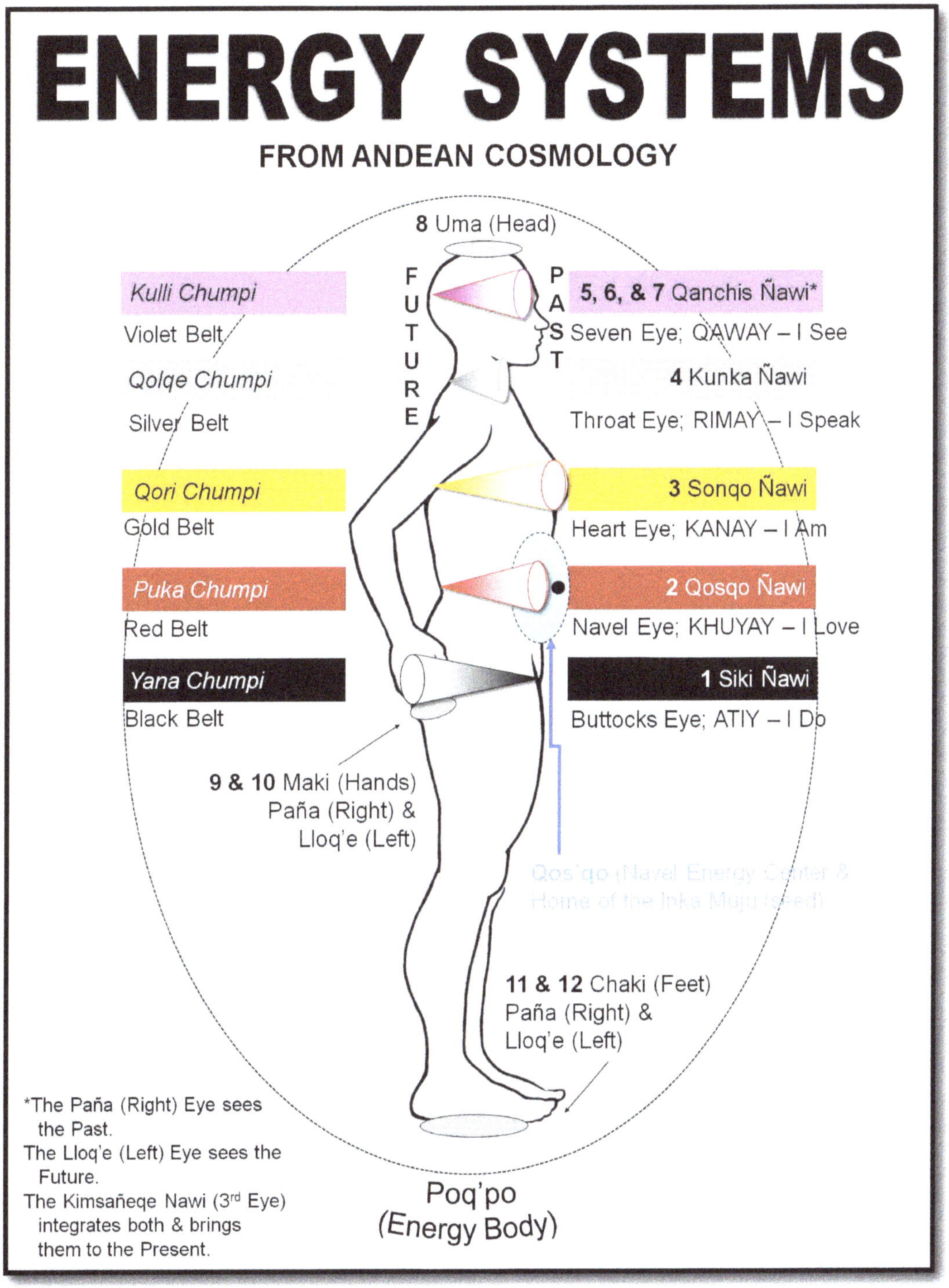

Below is a diagram that shows the *chumpikuna* (belts) of energy that surround the physical body.

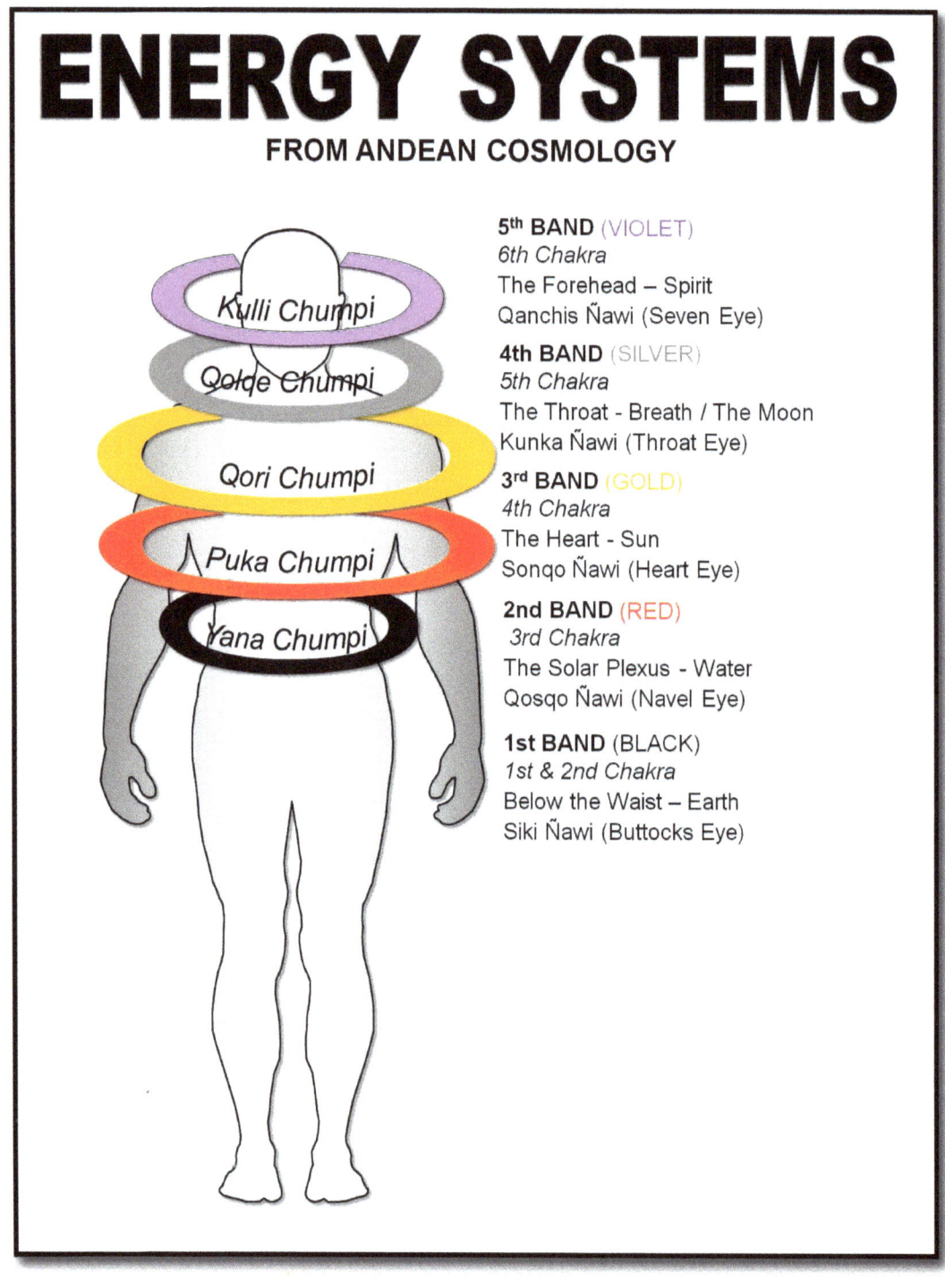

THE HINDU ENERGY SYSTEM

The *chakra* (disk, wheel, or cycle) system that Westerners are most familiar with originated from Hindu cosmology but also appears in Buddhist and Jain cosmologies. Seven major *chakras* are aligned along the spinal column and are connected by vertical channels of energy. This energy system is what connects the spiritual energy body to the physical material body when the soul is incarnated on the Earth plane. There are also many more *chakras* that appear in the hands, feet, below the feet, and above the head.

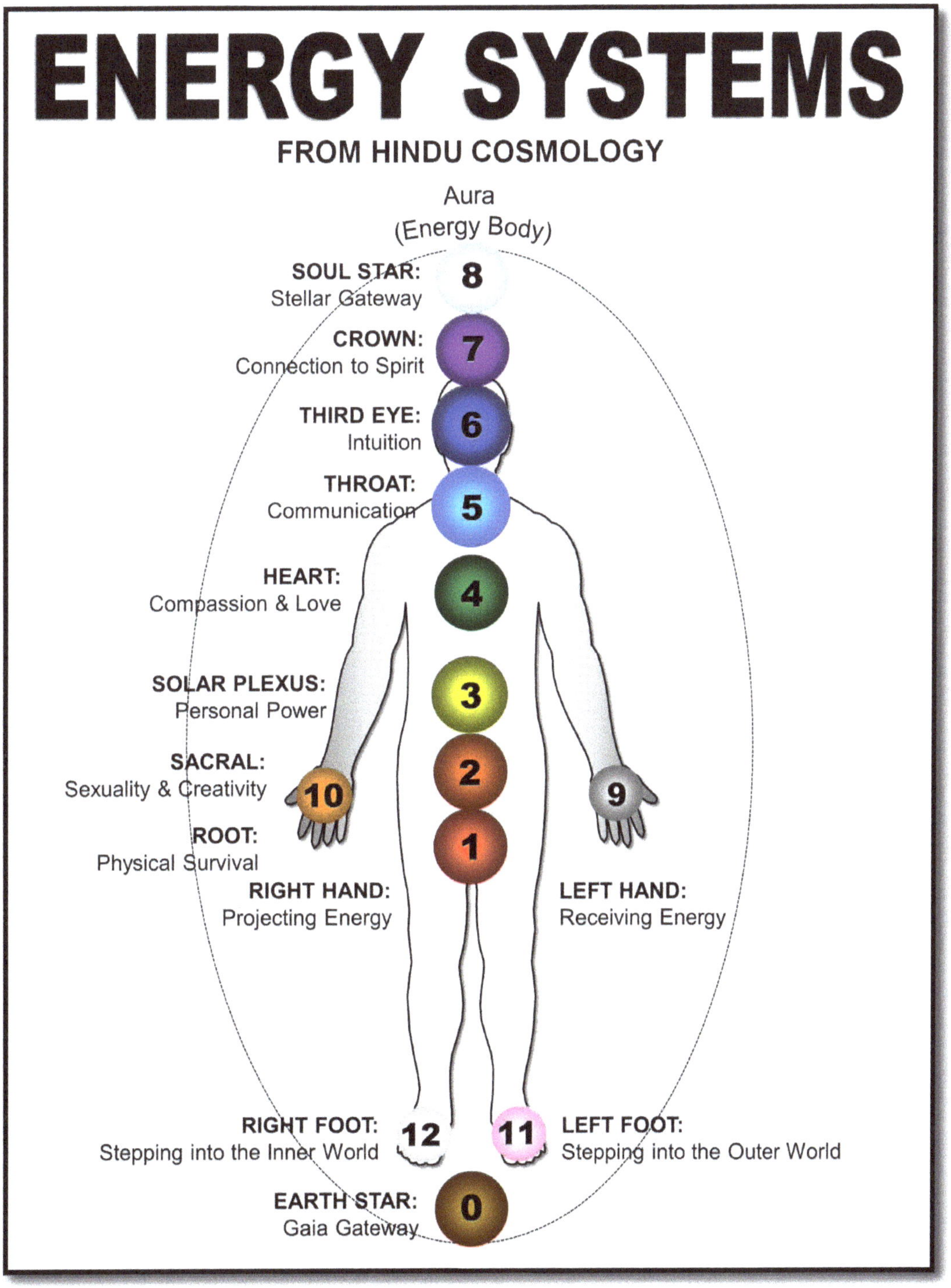

ENERGY SYSTEMS
FROM HINDU COSMOLOGY

Aura (Energy Body)

- **SOUL STAR:** Stellar Gateway — 8
- **CROWN:** Connection to Spirit — 7
- **THIRD EYE:** Intuition — 6
- **THROAT:** Communication — 5
- **HEART:** Compassion & Love — 4
- **SOLAR PLEXUS:** Personal Power — 3
- **SACRAL:** Sexuality & Creativity — 2
- **ROOT:** Physical Survival — 1
- **RIGHT HAND:** Projecting Energy — 10
- **LEFT HAND:** Receiving Energy — 9
- **RIGHT FOOT:** Stepping into the Inner World — 12
- **LEFT FOOT:** Stepping into the Outer World — 11
- **EARTH STAR:** Gaia Gateway — 0

Similar to the Andean energy system, the *chakras* attached to the physical body have cones of energy. However, unlike the Andean system, most of the cones are bi-directional, pointing both to the front and to the back of the body.

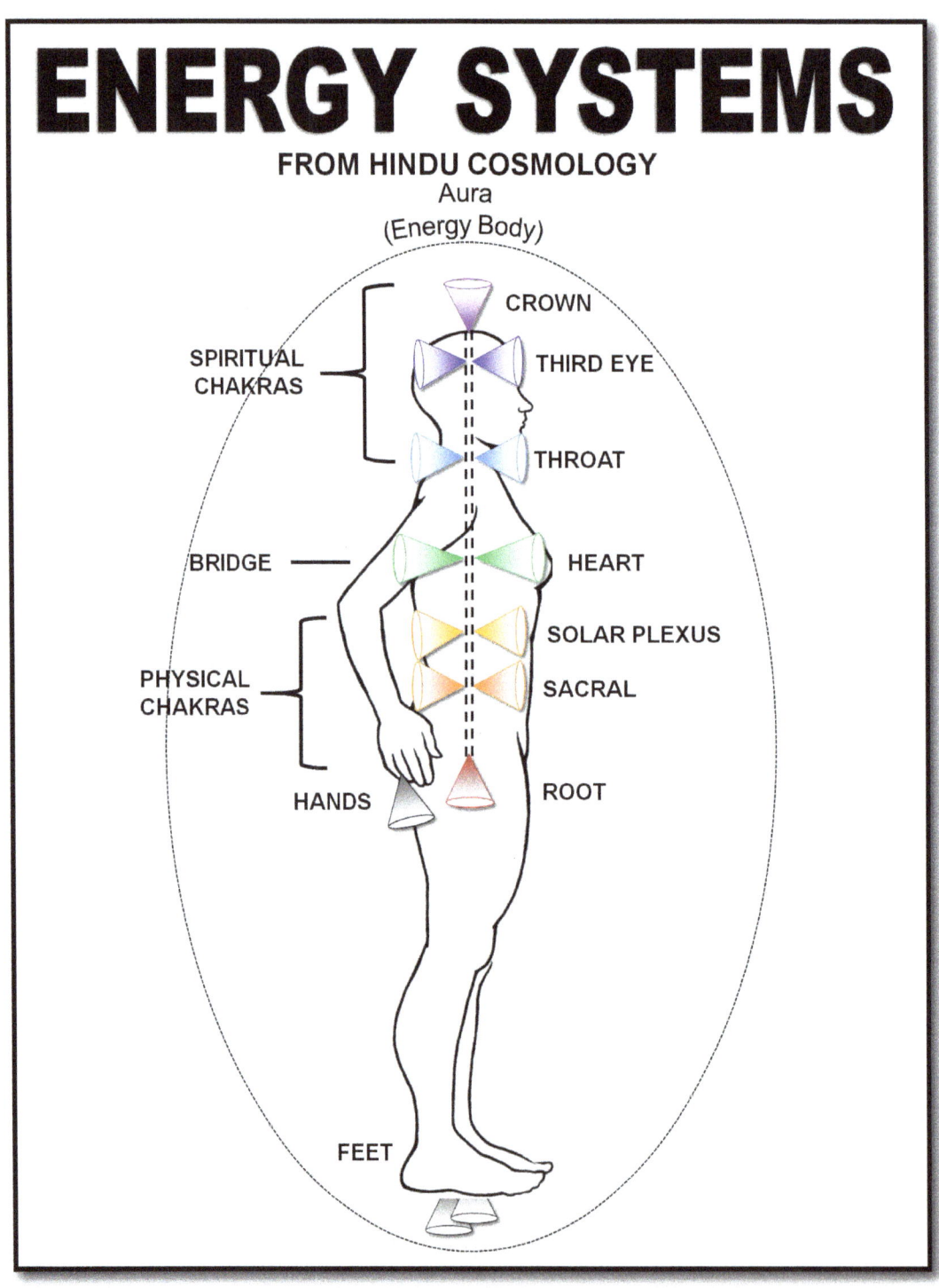

The energy channel that connects the *chakra* system is the *sushumna* along the spinal column. The *ida* and *pingala* also weave through the *chakra* system. Another similarity of the two energy systems is the *kundalini*, a coiled snake-like energy representing Divine Feminine Energy, that sits at the base of the spine. This is the same area that the Andean *Sach'amama* (Mama Tree in the form of a snake) is associated.

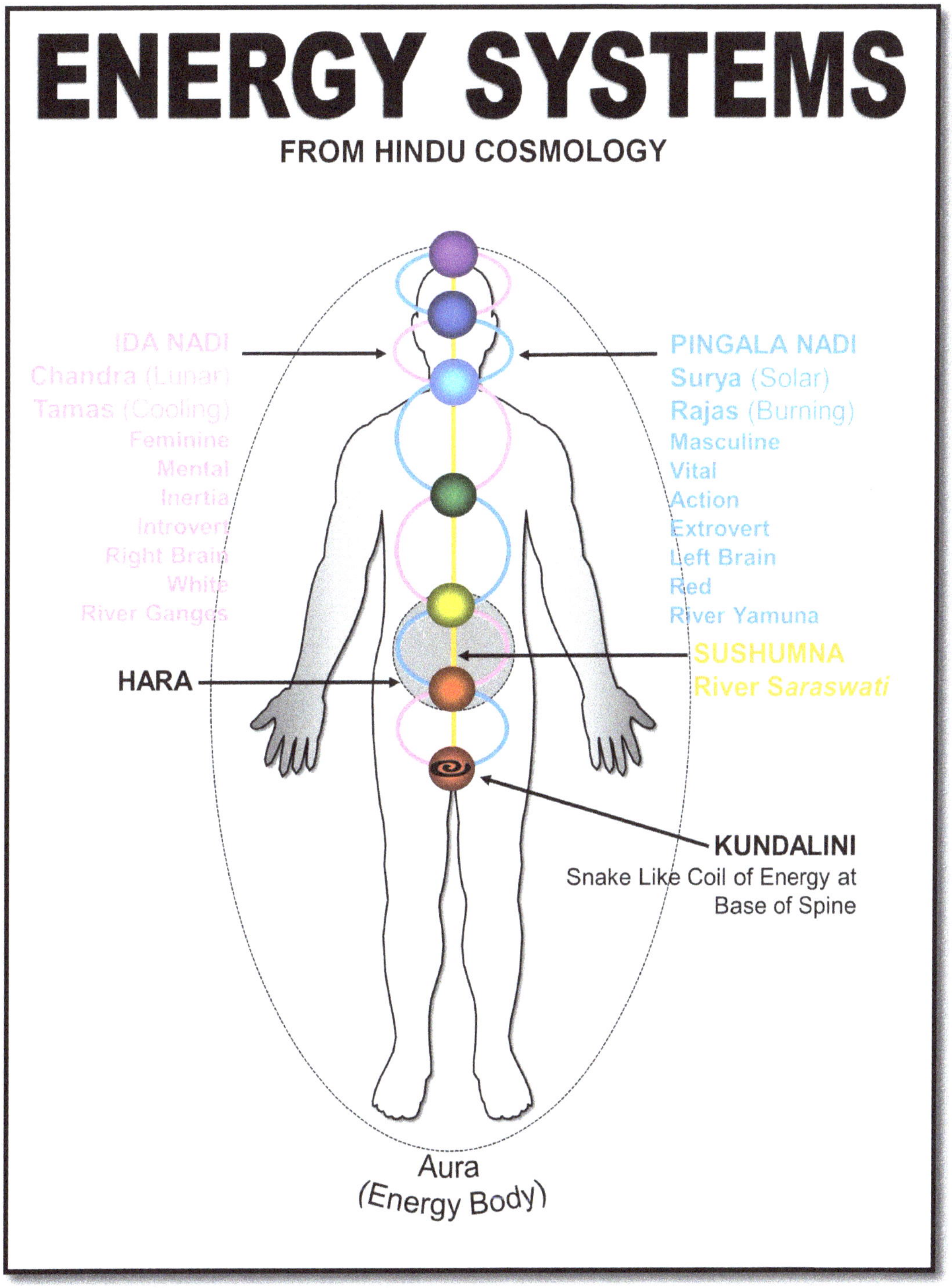

ENERGY SYSTEMS
FROM HINDU COSMOLOGY

IDA NADI
Chandra (Lunar)
Tamas (Cooling)
Feminine
Mental
Inertia
Introvert
Right Brain
White
River Ganges

PINGALA NADI
Surya (Solar)
Rajas (Burning)
Masculine
Vital
Action
Extrovert
Left Brain
Red
River Yamuna

SUSHUMNA
River *Saraswati*

HARA

KUNDALINI
Snake Like Coil of Energy at Base of Spine

Aura (Energy Body)

ENERGY TRANSMISSION WORK

A *karpay* or *qarpay* is a ceremony where living energy is invoked and transmitted from one individual, the *paq'o* (Andean medicine person), to another individual. The energy is sourced from the Andean ancestor lineage. *Karpay* literally means "irrigation" or "watering". Elizabeth B. Jenkins, in her book, *The Fourth Level: Nature Wisdom Teachings of the Inka*, says that the purpose of *karpay* is to water an individual's Inka *muju* (energy seed) so that it can sprout.

Paq'okuna usually develop their own style of *karpay*. They may also require that the receiving individual perform some prerequisite training or self-development. *Chumpi* stones are used in a few of these *karpay* rituals, which are described below.

Alberto Villoldo, author of many books including the classic *Shaman, Healer, Sage*, is a medical anthropologist who studied with the Q'ero in Peru. When he returned to the United States, he began The Four Winds Shamanic School, where many Andean concepts of energy medicine are taught. The school teaches a *karpay* system call the *Munay Ki* Rites.

Munay means "heart" and *Ki* means "energy" or "motion". Together, *Munay Ki* becomes the energy of unconditional love in motion. The intention of the rites is to plant seeds in the energy fields of the *chakras* to allow them to glow creating a rainbow body. Altogether there are a total of nine unique *Munay Ki* rites.

There are two rites in which the *chumpi* stones are used:

THE CHUMPI AWAY (ah-way) **KARPAY** is a traditional Andean karpay. This rite is also used in the Westernized *Munay Ki* tradition, where it is called the "Bands of Power Rite". This rite weaves (*away*) the energy bands surrounding the physical body to offer protection from any unwanted energies. It works with the Andean energy body, which is composed of five major bands.

THE AYNI KARPAY is called the "Harmony Rite" in the *Munay Ki* tradition. It installs an Andean archetype to each *chakra*. This rite works with the Hindu energy body, adopted by the Western world, which is composed of seven major *chakras*.

Below I will describe the process of each of these rites that use the *chumpi* stones but it is not intended as a guide of how to give these rites. Learning about the rites is a good introduction to the Andean cosmology of the energy body. After reading this section you may be inspired to receive these rites. There are many shamanic practitioners that have been trained to give *karpays* in the traditional method or to give the *Munay Ki* as taught by The Four Winds school.

Chumpi Away – The Munay Ki Bands of Power Rite

The intention of this *karpay* is to fine tune energetic protection for the body. In Andean cosmology there are five bands of energy that surround the physical body. Each one has a *ñawi* (eye) in the center of the band. Five *chumpi* stones are used to weave (*away* in Quechua) the bands together to form a protective shield around the physical body. The bands are:

YANA CHUMPI (Black Band) – This band represents the rich dark *allpa* (earth), where the seeds of becoming are planted. The black band is located below the waist. Its eye is called the

"*Siki Ñawi* (Tail Eye)". This eye is the only one to point out the back of the physical body and is considered the first *chakra*. The number one *chumpi* stone is used to weave this band.

PUKA CHUMPI (Red Band) – This band represents the band of *unu* (water), which is the life blood for *Pachamama* (Mother Earth). Water falls on the earth to nourish it. The red band is located at the solar plexus area. Its eye is called the "*Qosqo Ñawi* (Navel Eye)". This eye points out the front of the physical body and is considered the second *chakra*. The number two *chumpi* stone is used to weave this band.

QORI CHUMPI (Gold Band) – This band represents *inti* (the sun), that shines on the earth to support the seed's growth. The gold band is located at the heart area. Its eye is called the "*Songo Ñawi* (Heart Eye)". This eye also points out the front of the physical body and is considered the third *chakra*. The number three *chumpi* stone is used to weave this band.

QOLQE CHUMPI (Silver Band) – This band represents *killa* (the moon) as well as *wayra* (wind). Wind gives our voice power. The silver band is located at the throat area. Its eye is called the "*Kunka Ñawi* (Throat Eye)". This eye also points out the front of the physical body and is considered the fourth *chakra*. The number four *chumpi* stone is used to weave this band.

KULLI CHUMPI (Violet Band) – This band represents *Nuna* (Spirit), where all things are possible. The violet band is located at the forehead area. Its eye is called the "*Qanchis Ñawi* (Seven Eye)". This eye also points out the front of the physical body. The right eye, left eye, and third eye are considered the fifth, sixth, and seventh *chakras*. The number five *chumpi* stone is used to weave this band.

Note: Some medicine people may describe this band as white, clear, or the color of the receiving individual's eyes.

Together the bands create a rainbow of energy that cascades down from the crown filling the energy body with energy. Additionally, each band has *qori* (gold) and *qolqe* (silver) threads that run down into the ground.

CHUMPI BAND	1	2	3	4	5
Body Area	Stomach	Solar Plexus	Heart	Throat	Forehead
Color	Black	Red	Gold	Silver	Violet
Symbol For	Earth	Water	Fire (Sun)	Moon & Wind (Breath)	Spirit (White Light)

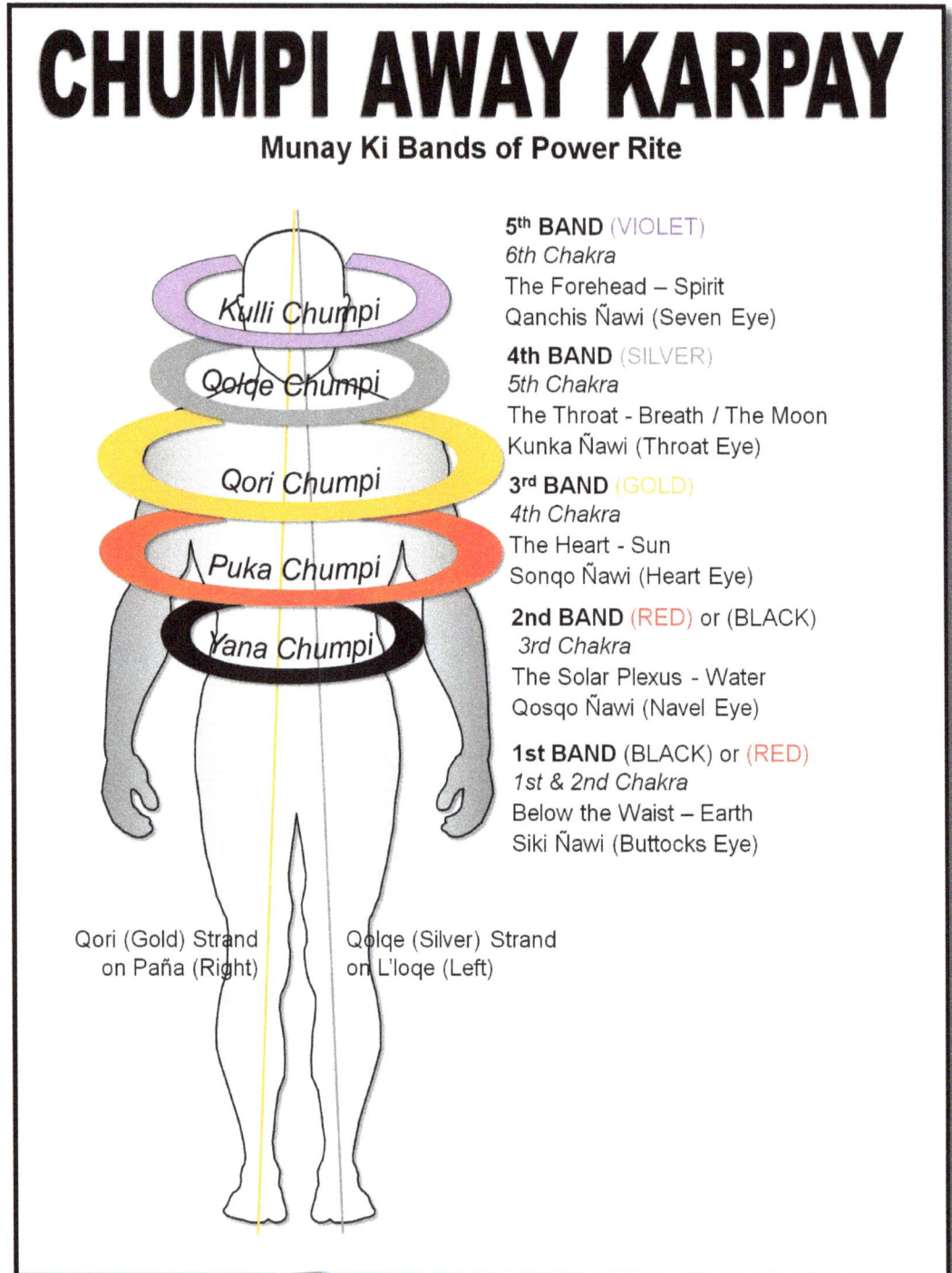

Ayni Karpay – The Munay Ki Harmony Rite

This energy transmission installs the seeds of seven Andean archetypes into the seven *chakra*s (based on Hindu cosmology). These seeds are germinated by fire ceremony that awakens them so that they can create *chakra*s full of light. Seven *chumpi* stones can be used to install archetypes into the seven major *chakra*s of the physical body. Optionally, an eighth *chumpi* stone can be used to install an archetype into the *chakra* of the energy body located above the crown. Four animal archetypes are transmitted to the first four *chakra*s and four luminous beings are transmitted to the upper four. These archetypes are:

SACH'AMAMA (Serpent or Snake) – *Sach'amama* literally means Mother Tree but appears in Andean/Amazon cosmology as a 2-headed snake. It represents the lowest *chakra* because it is the closest to the earth, crawling along on its belly. In Andean cosmology it is the animal keeper of the *Ukhupacha* (Lower World). The number one *chumpi* stone is used to install the archetype of this chakra.

PUMA (Cougar) or OTORONGO / CHINCHAY (Jaguar) – *Puma* or *Otorongo* is the big cat that walks in its power. It represents the second *chakra* which is a part of the power center in the physical body. In Andean cosmology it is the animal keeper of the *Kaypacha* (Middle World). The number two *chumpi* stone is used to install the archetype of this chakra.

Q'ENTI (Hummingbird) – *Q'enti* is the hummingbird that sips sweet nectar. Hummingbird represents the third *chakra* which is also part of the power center in the physical body. The hummingbird is revered in Andean cosmology as a psychopomp. It is called *siwar q'enti* (royal hummingbird) and has the ability to fly between the three shamanic worlds and cross pollinate them. The number three *chumpi* stone is used to install the archetype of this chakra.

KUNTUR (Condor) – *Kuntur* is the condor that flies so high in the sky. Condor represents the fourth *chakra* which is the heart center. In Andean cosmology it is the animal keeper of the *Hanaqpacha* (Upper World). The number four *chumpi* stone is used to install the archetype of this chakra.

HUASCÁR INKA – Huascár was the twelfth ruler of the Inka Empire before the Spanish conquistadors invaded and usurped Inka power. He represents the fifth *chakra*. He is the human keeper of the *Ukhupacha* (Lower World). The number five *chumpi* stone is used to install the archetype of this chakra.

Note: Historical sources will cite Huascár's half-brother, Atahualpa, as the last Inka ruler. However, he murdered Huascár to steal the title and did it during the Spanish invasion. He, in turn, was beheaded by the Spaniards, then was succeeded by six more Inka rulers however they all were essentially puppets of the Spaniards.

MANCO CAPÁK – Legend says that Manco Capák, with his wife Mama Ocllo, emerged from Lake Titicaca to found Cusco and the Inka Empire. He became the first Inka ruler. He represents the sixth *chakra* which is the psychic center in the physical body. He is called "the son of the Sun" and is chosen as the human keeper of the *Kaypacha* (Middle World). The number six *chumpi* stone is used to install the archetype of this chakra.

Note: The Four Winds School teaches Quetzalcoatl, the feathered serpent, should be installed in the sixth *chakra*. He was from Meso-American cosmology and not an Inka so I am not certain why he is used. I choose to install Manco Capác, who began the Inka lineage. He seems quite appropriate to represent the Middle World.

PACHAKUTI INKA – Pachakuti was the ninth Inka ruler and was named "The Transformer of the World" and "Earthshaker". He is credited with building Machu Picchu and rebuilding Cusco. He represents the seventh *chakra* which is the spiritual center in the physical body. He is the human keeper of the *Hanaqpacha* (Upper World). The number seven *chumpi* stone is used to install the archetype of this chakra.

Note: *Pachakuti* also means a turning inside out and turning upside down of our world, a revolution of time and space. The Inka believe in a succession of cycles of time. There is a cataclysmic event, a *pachakuti*, that occurs at the end of each cycle, approximately every 500 years.

WIRAQOCHA – Wiraqocha was the eighth Inka ruler. He represents the eighth *chakra* which is in the energy body above the crown *chakra*. Wiraqocha literally means "foam of the sea". He was also a Creator God of the Sun and Storms in the Aymara culture centered around Lake Titicaca. Legend says that Wiraqocha rose from Lake Titicaca during darkness to bring forth light. His son was Inti (Sun), his daughter was Killa (Moon), and his wife was Mama Qocha (Lake). He was also known by other names such as Huaracocha, Con, Con Ticci (Kon Tiki), Thunupa, Taapac, Tupaca and Illa (Light). The Wiracochas were an ancient culture that built Tiwanako. The deity above their famous gate is that of Wiraqocha. The number eight *chumpi* stone is used to install the archetype of this chakra.

CHAKRA & CHUMPI #	ANDEAN ARCHETYPE	ENGLISH ARCHETYPE	QUALITY
1	Sach'amama	Serpent or Snake	Connection to the Earth
2	Puma or Otorongo	Jaguar	Sensing & Power
3	Q'ente	Hummingbird	Joy & Passion
4	Kuntur	Condor or Eagle	Strength & Courage
5	Huascár Inka	Last Inka Ruler	Keeper of the Lower World (Unconscious)
6	Manco Capák	Founder of Cusco & the Inka Lineage	Keeper of the Middle World (Conscious)
7	Pachakuti Inka	9th Inka Ruler & Transformer of the World	Keeper of the Upper World (Superconscious)
8	Wiraqocha	The Source of All that Is	Connection to the Cosmos

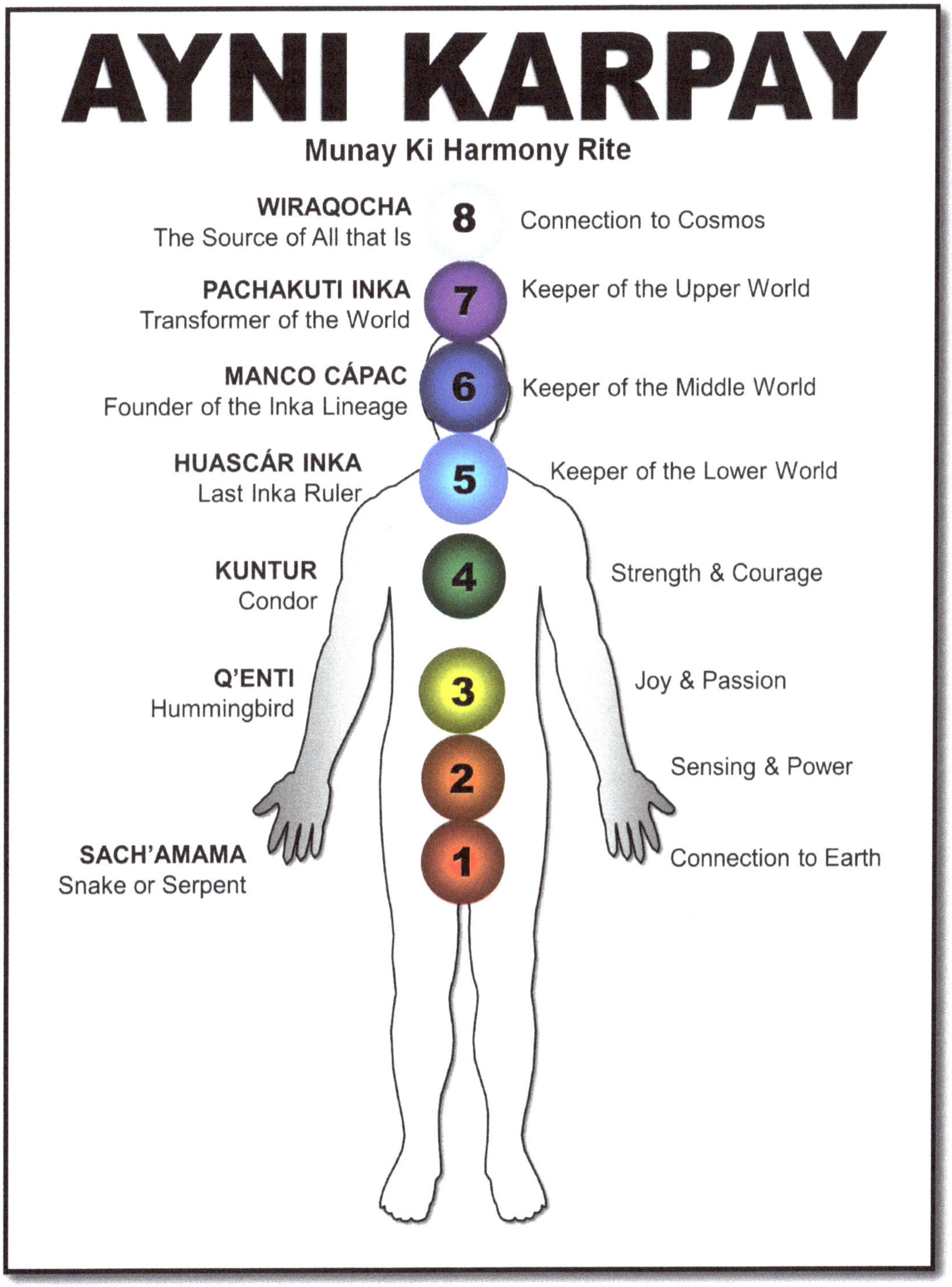

AYNI KARPAY
Munay Ki Harmony Rite

WIRAQOCHA — The Source of All that Is — 8 — Connection to Cosmos

PACHAKUTI INKA — Transformer of the World — 7 — Keeper of the Upper World

MANCO CÁPAC — Founder of the Inka Lineage — 6 — Keeper of the Middle World

HUASCÁR INKA — Last Inka Ruler — 5 — Keeper of the Lower World

KUNTUR — Condor — 4 — Strength & Courage

Q'ENTI — Hummingbird — 3 — Joy & Passion

— 2 — Sensing & Power

SACH'AMAMA — Snake or Serpent — 1 — Connection to Earth

HEALING WITH CHUMPI STONES

Chumpi stones can be used to extract *hucha* (dense energy) from the *poq'po* (energy body) or to direct *sami* (high vibratory energy) into the energy body. You set the desired intention as you work with the stones. They are used to form energetic patterns or grids. *Chumpi* stone grids can be used for yourself or for friends, family, and clients. You may want to experiment with creating a grid around your bed so that energy shifts as you sleep. Or try creating a grid around your work area for protection and balance.

If you plan to use *chumpi* stones as a tool for helping others, here is a process I use. As in all things, adapt and adjust this process to fit your intentions and style.

1. Begin by creating a safe and sacred space in which to work.

2. Ask the client to express a specific goal for their session.

3. Choose an Andean textile (if available), that will support the goal of the client. You can rely on messages from your guides as well as your own intuition to assist in choosing the right tools to support the goal of the session. (Refer to the Textile Correspondences on pages 25.)

    For example: I might choose a symbol that will bring the client into balance or put them in right relationship. I use a 2-panel cloth to provide calming energy through solid colors. I use a 4-panel cloth to provide foundation and stability. I use an *inti* (sun) symbol to connect to masculine energy or to illuminate an issue. I use a *ch'ily qocha* (body of water) pattern to connect to feminine energy or fluidity. I use a cloth with a lot of *pallay* (pattern) to stir up or call-in energy. I use woven *ñawi* (eyes) for clarity of vision. I use a *k'uychi* (rainbow) cloth for inclusivity or balance. I use the *pallay tukuy* (finishing design) on a cloth to finish or close an issue. I use the *tawa inti qocha* (four lake sun) symbol to work with the energies of the cycles of time. I use the *apu* (mountain) symbol to connect the energies of the terrestrial to the celestial. I use the *chakana* (Southern Cross) cloth to provide guidance and direction. I use the *ch'unchu* (wild jungle dancer) symbol to connect the client to their roots and their origin.

4. Create a *chumpi* stone grid around the client (either on the body, beside the body, or on the floor beneath them if you are using a massage table).

5. With the *chumpi* grid in place, perform your energy work, which may include: clearing the *chakras*, unblocking the energy pathways, cleaning and smoothing the aura, cutting unwanted cords, and creating a good grounding system. It is very important to scan and remove any foreign, stagnant, or heavy energy from the *poq'po* (energy body). Use the tools you usually work with to move energy such as: Florida water, sage smudge sticks, feather fans, tuning forks, bells, colored lights, crystals, etc.

    Two Andean healing techniques can also be used. *Pichay* (to clean, sweep, or erase) is the action of moving energy through the *poq'po* (energy body) by using a feather fan, *mesa* (sacred bundle), *despacho* (offering bundle), or *chumpi* stone. *Tupanaqui* (to tap) is the action of moving heavy energy away from the *poq'po* by repeatedly tapping two stones together throughout the energy field.

If you are familiar with Andean healing, create a *saiwa* (column of energy) that originates at *Pachamama* (Mother Earth), moves through the *chumpi* stone grid, up through the symbolism on the textile, then through the *poq'po*, toward the Cosmos. This informs the *poq'po* by imprinting it with high vibratory energy patterns.

6. Close your session in your usual way of working. I usually end with doing Reiki to stabilize all of the shifts in energy that occurred during the session. Also insure that your client is fully present and grounded after receiving energy work and before releasing them from your space.

GRIDS FOR HEALING WORK

Below I offer four alternatives for *chumpi* stone grids to use in energy work. You can create these grids for yourself or use them for friends, family members, and clients. Try all of the variations yourself to compare the differences in the energy.

1-Point Chakra Layout

A single stone or an entire set of stones can be placed directly on a *chakra*. *Hiwaya* (meteorite stone) *chumpi* stones are very powerful energetic magnets that are good energy cleansers. They are used to open the *chakras*, suck out *hucha*, and then close them. Choose a *chakra* that needs repair. Place all of the stones on that *chakra* as you perform your usual energy medicine routine.

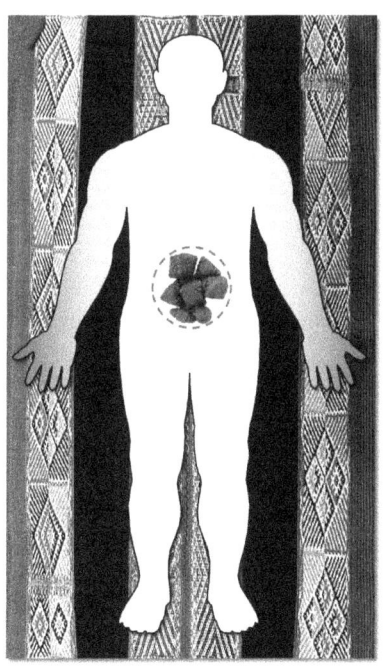

5-Point Star Layout

The 5-pointed star represents the human figure, that has five senses, five fingers on a hand, five toes on a foot, and five extremities. The body is composed of five parts of equal length from top to bottom: the head, chest, pelvis, thigh, and leg. It is also composed of five parts of equal length cross wise: with arms outstretched, hand to chest to other hand, hand to elbow and elbow to shoulder.

The 5-pointed star is also a symbol represented in many pagan spiritual traditions. It is the meeting point of heaven with earth that includes four cardinal points plus the center point. It also represents the five elements of the Western world (fire, earth, air, water, and spirit or ether) as well as the five elements in Chinese cosmology (fire, earth, metal, water, and wood).

Use this grid when you want to work with the energies of the human body. All the major points of the body are connected within this grid.

To create this grid, place one *chumpi* stone at the head, one at each of the hands, and one at each of the feet as shown in the diagram. It does not matter which *chumpi* number goes in each position but I usually place them clockwise in an ascending numerical order.

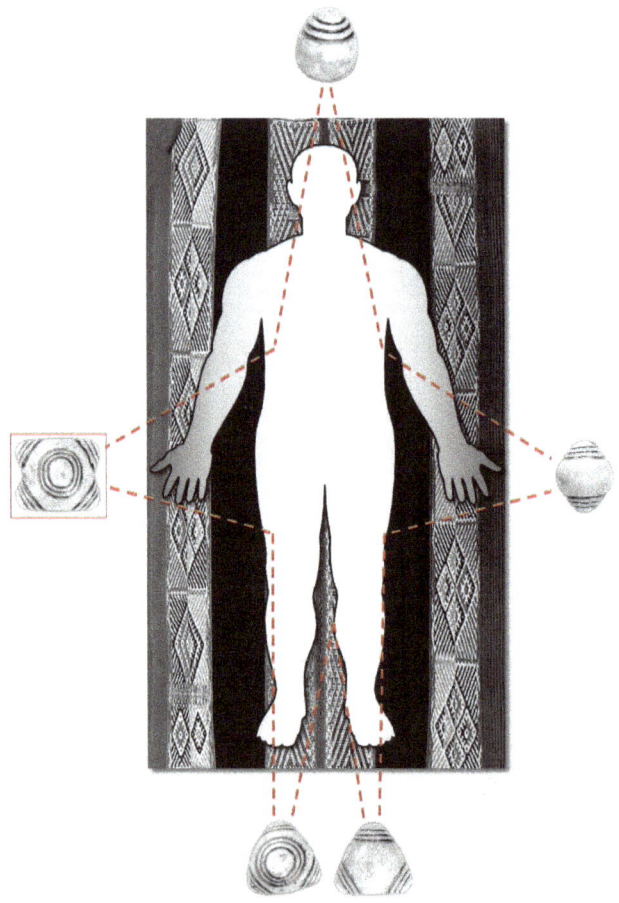

6-Point Star Layout

The first six *chumpi* stones are used to form the Star of David, which is a 6-pointed star that represents wholeness. The upward pointing triangle represents *Yin* and the downward triangle, *Yang*. Together they represent the union of the Divine Masculine and Feminine. The center point, where the two triangles intersect, represents the balance between dualities and is the merge point of matter and spirit. You can place a seventh *chumpi* stone at this point. This point usually is at the heart, *hara*, *qosqo*, or assemblage point area.

The *merkaba* is a 3-dimensional 6-pointed star with counter-rotating fields of light and energy that surrounds a soul. The *merkaba* is the Light Body which the soul uses as a vehicle of transportation in other dimensions. The word "*merkaba*" means "chariot" in Hebrew and is composed of three separate words: "mer" means connecting thread of Light, "ka" means The Spirit or Astral Self, and "ba" means The Body or Physical Self. With all of its symbolism, the *Merkaba* Grid is a very powerful one to work within.

Use this grid when you want to work with the energies of the divine feminine and divine masculine or use it as a vehicle to move consciousness for work in other dimensions.

To create this grid, place one *chumpi* stone at the head, one at the feet. Then place a stone at each of the four corners as shown in the diagram.

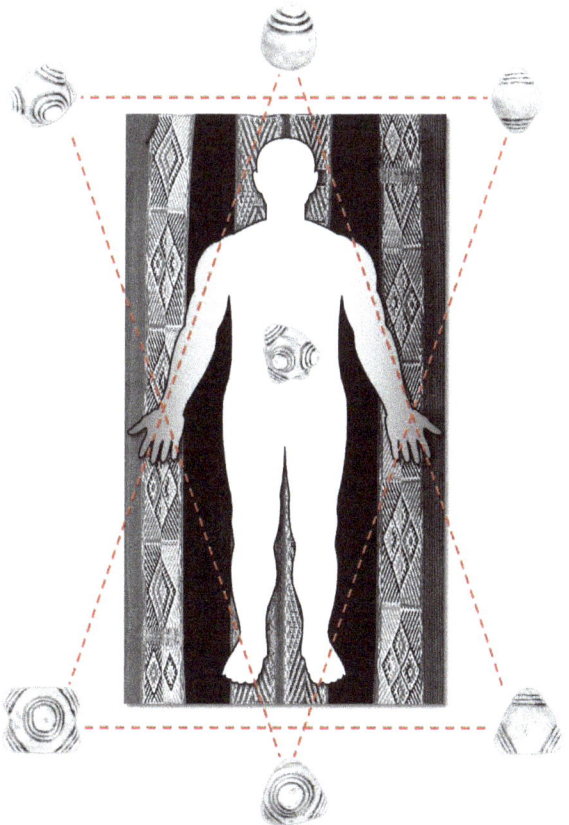

12-Point Chakana Layout

The *chakana* is a graphic design of the Southern Cross constellation in the Southern Hemisphere. The three steps represent the three shamanic worlds. The four flat sides represent the four elements. The central circle represents a portal to other dimensions. There are twelve corners around the outside of the *chakana*.

Use this grid when you want to work with the maximum number of *chumpi* stone points. It is also a good set up to connect to the celestial as you lie on the terrestrial.

To create this grid, place one *chumpi* stone at each corner of an imaginary outline of the *chakana* symbol as shown in the diagram.

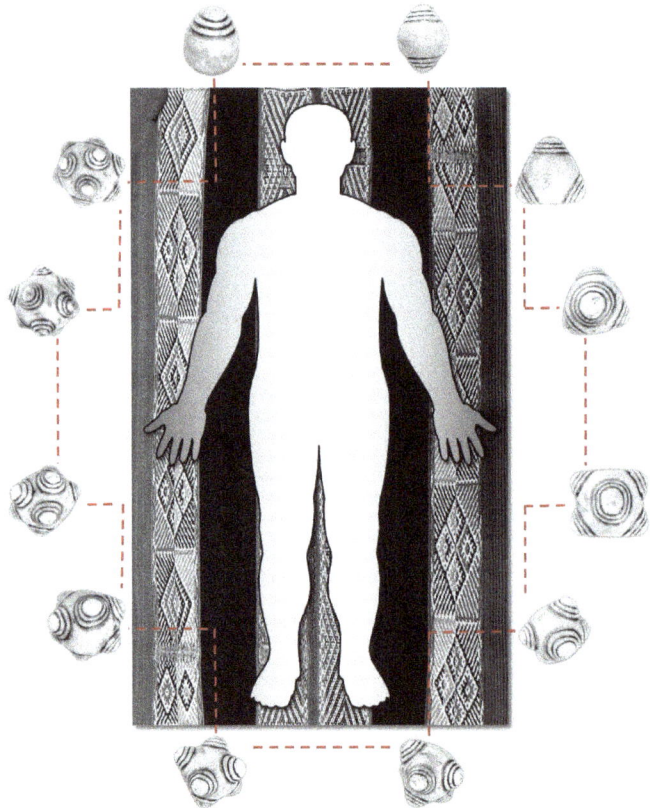

APPENDIXES

CHUMPI STONE WORKSHEET

Date: _____

Chumpi Stone Number or Name: _____

Inquiry/Question: _____

Message from Chumpi Stone: _____

Chumpi Stone Correspondence Notes: _____

_____

_____

_____

_____

_____

_____

_____

_____

_____

_____

This worksheet can be downloaded from www.ChumpiSacredStones.com

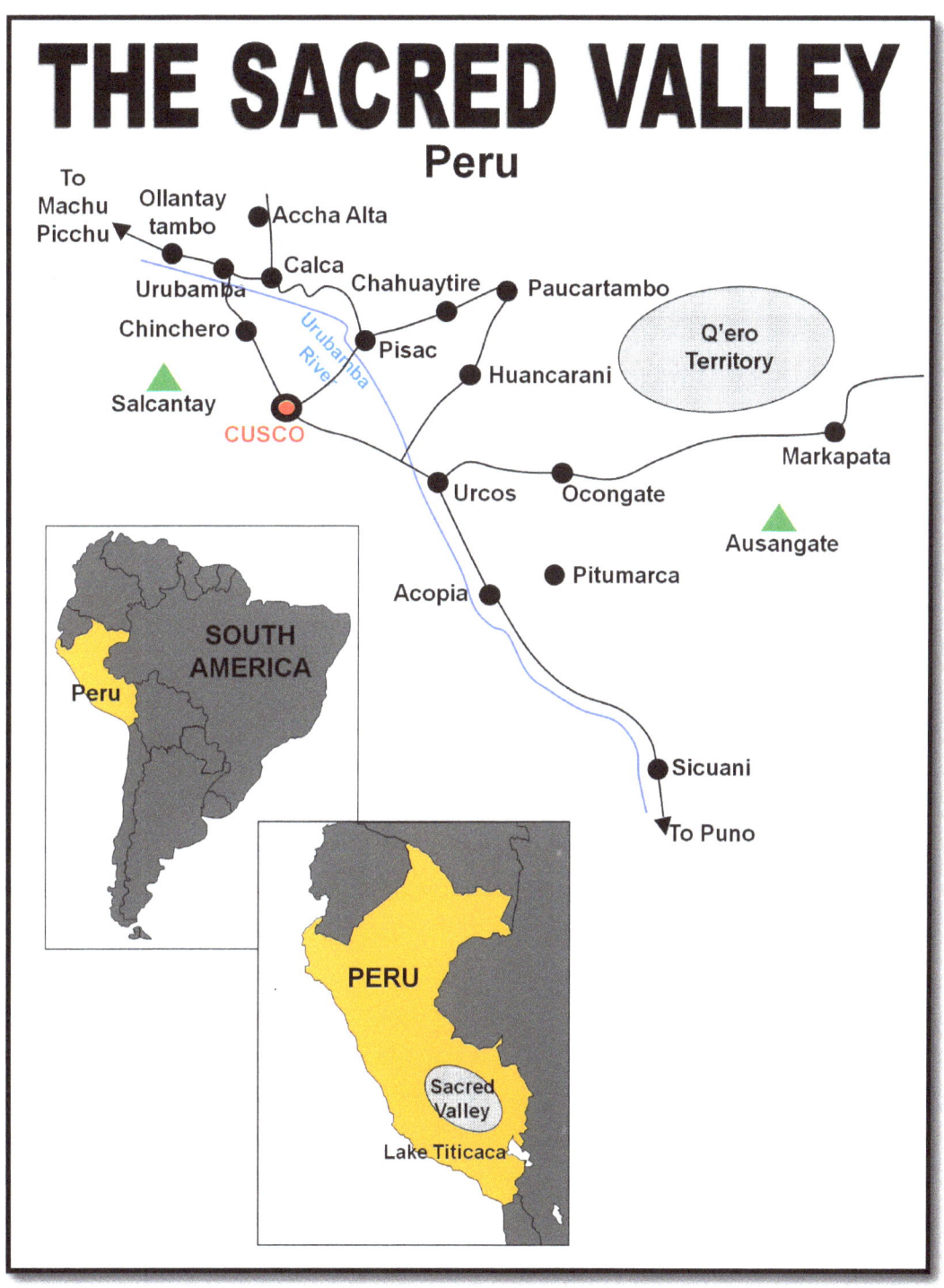

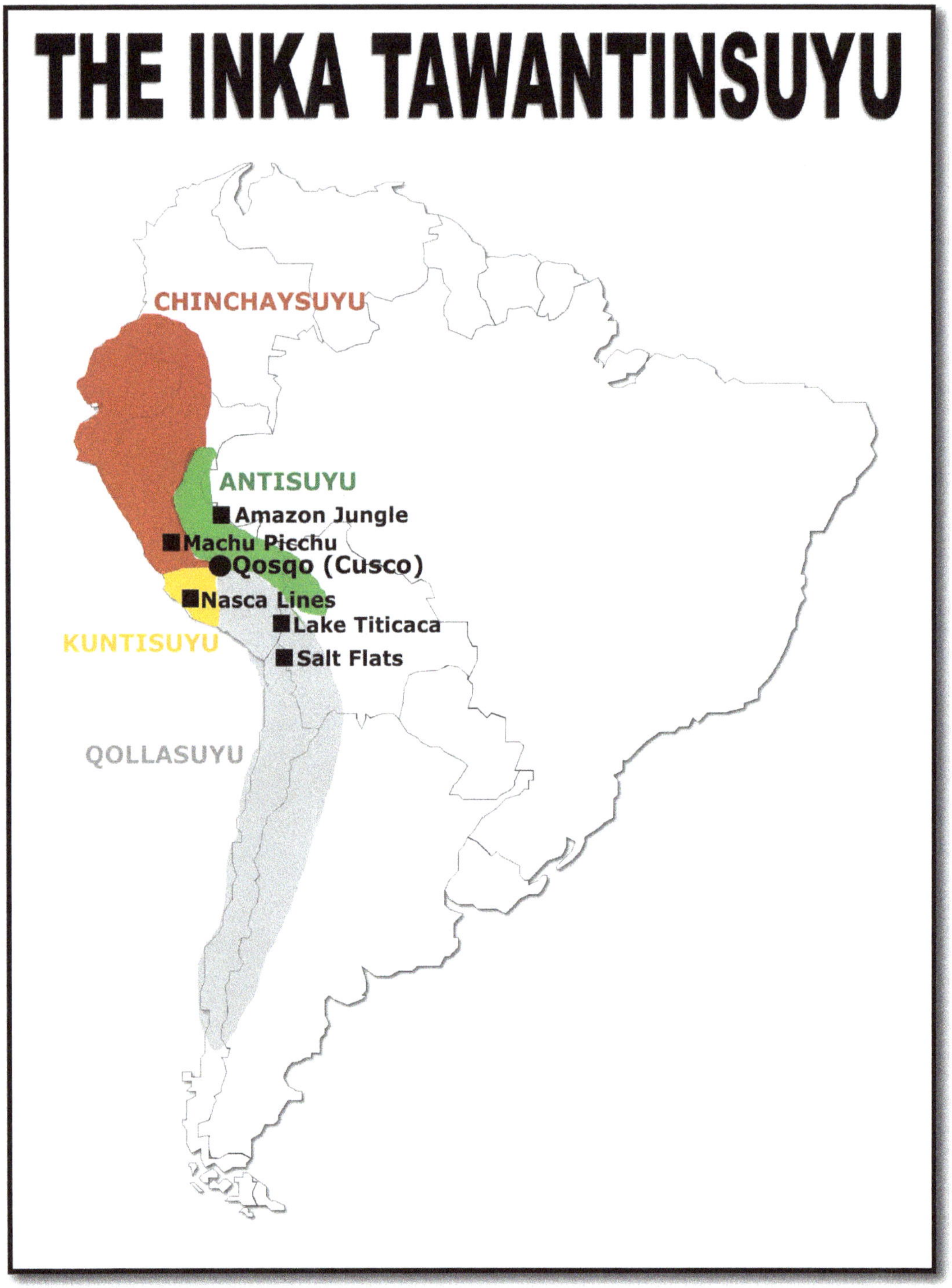

THE INKA TAWANTINSUYU

- CHINCHAYSUYU
- ANTISUYU
  - Amazon Jungle
  - Machu Picchu
  - Qosqo (Cusco)
  - Nasca Lines
  - Lake Titicaca
  - Salt Flats
- KUNTISUYU
- QOLLASUYU

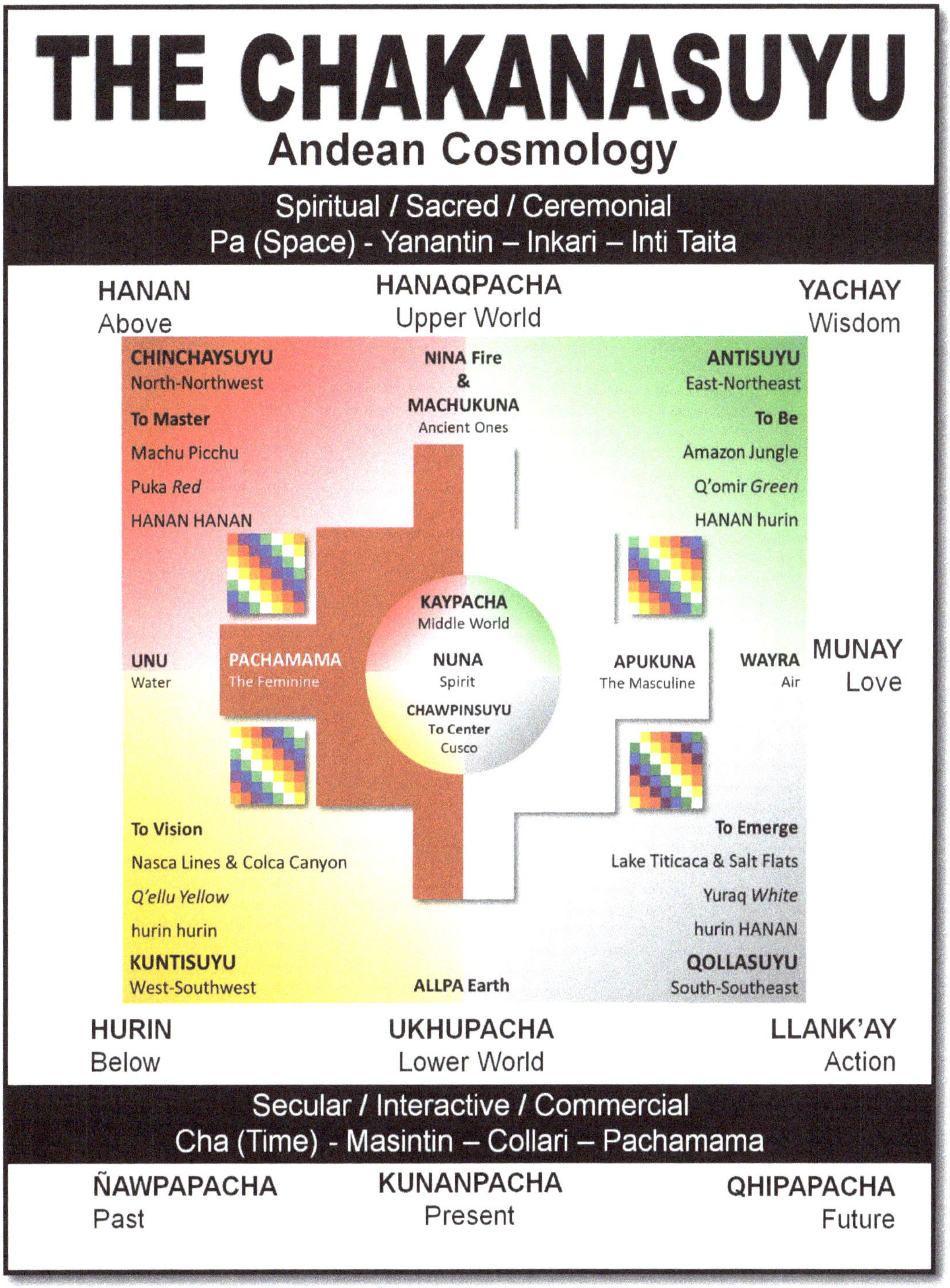

THE CHAKANASUYU
Andean Cosmology

Spiritual / Sacred / Ceremonial
Pa (Space) - Yanantin – Inkari – Inti Taita

HANAN — Above
HANAQPACHA — Upper World
YACHAY — Wisdom

CHINCHAYSUYU
North-Northwest
To Master
Machu Picchu
Puka *Red*
HANAN HANAN

**NINA Fire &
MACHUKUNA**
Ancient Ones

ANTISUYU
East-Northeast
To Be
Amazon Jungle
Q'omir *Green*
HANAN hurin

KAYPACHA
Middle World

UNU
Water

PACHAMAMA
The Feminine

NUNA
Spirit
CHAWPINSUYU
To Center
Cusco

APUKUNA
The Masculine

WAYRA
Air

MUNAY — Love

To Vision
Nasca Lines & Colca Canyon
Q'ellu *Yellow*
hurin hurin
KUNTISUYU
West-Southwest

ALLPA Earth

To Emerge
Lake Titicaca & Salt Flats
Yuraq *White*
hurin HANAN
QOLLASUYU
South-Southeast

HURIN — Below
UKHUPACHA — Lower World
LLANK'AY — Action

Secular / Interactive / Commercial
Cha (Time) - Masintin – Collari – Pachamama

ÑAWPAPACHA — Past
KUNANPACHA — Present
QHIPAPACHA — Future

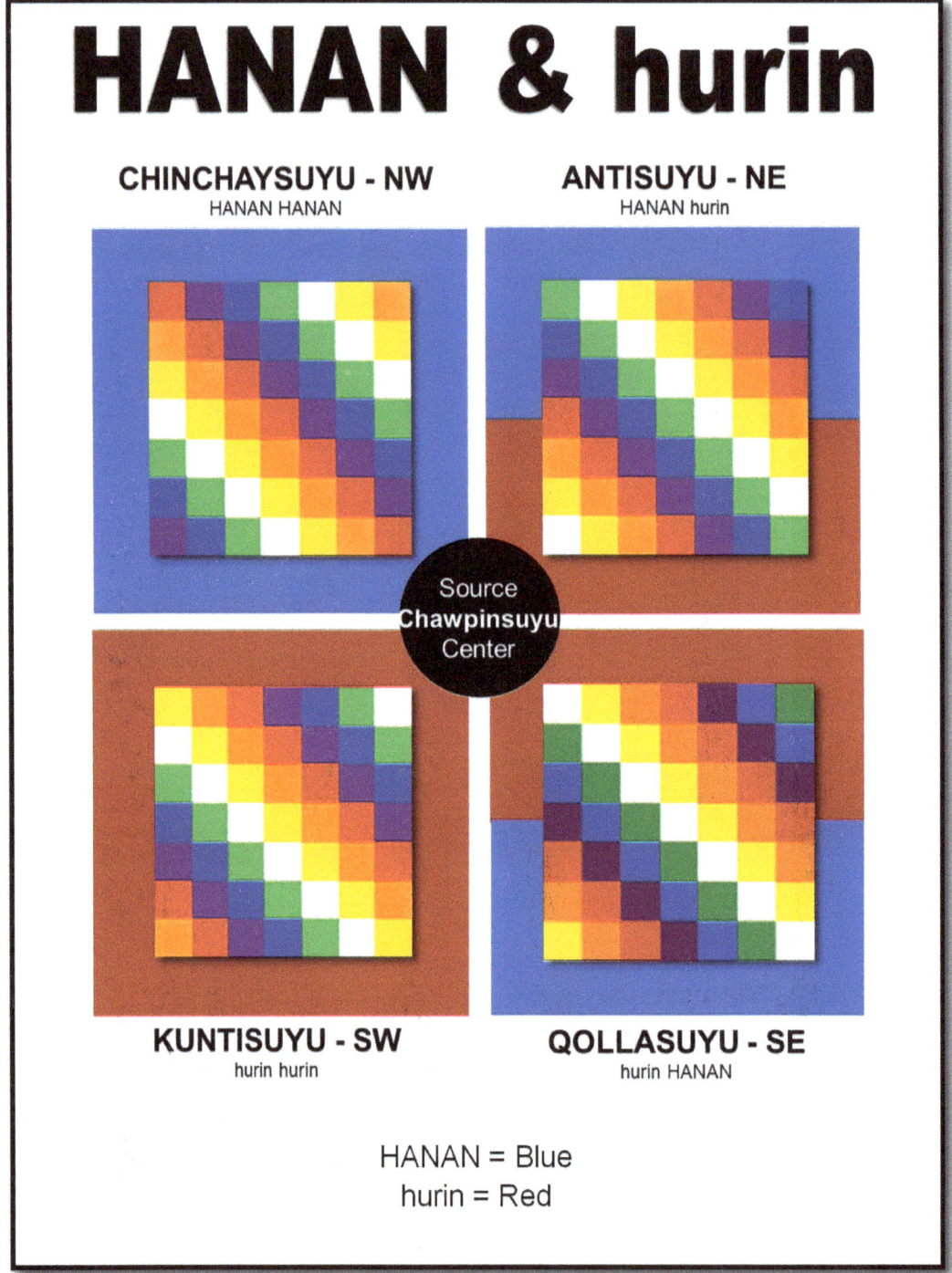

HANAN (upper part) and *hurin* (lower part) are energy concepts that permeate Inka cosmology. Cusco, the capital of the Inka Empire, was even designed in the shape of a jaguar, with a designated upper part, the HANAN, and a lower part, the hurin. The following table lists attributes associated with *HANAN* and *hurin*:

HANAN	hurin
HANAN (Upper, Above, Superior)	hurin (Lower, Below, Inferior)
Willka, Nunapukacha (Sacred, Spiritual World)	Kaypacha (Secular, Physical World)
Hanaqpacha (Sky, Celestial)	Pachamama (Earth, Terrestrial)

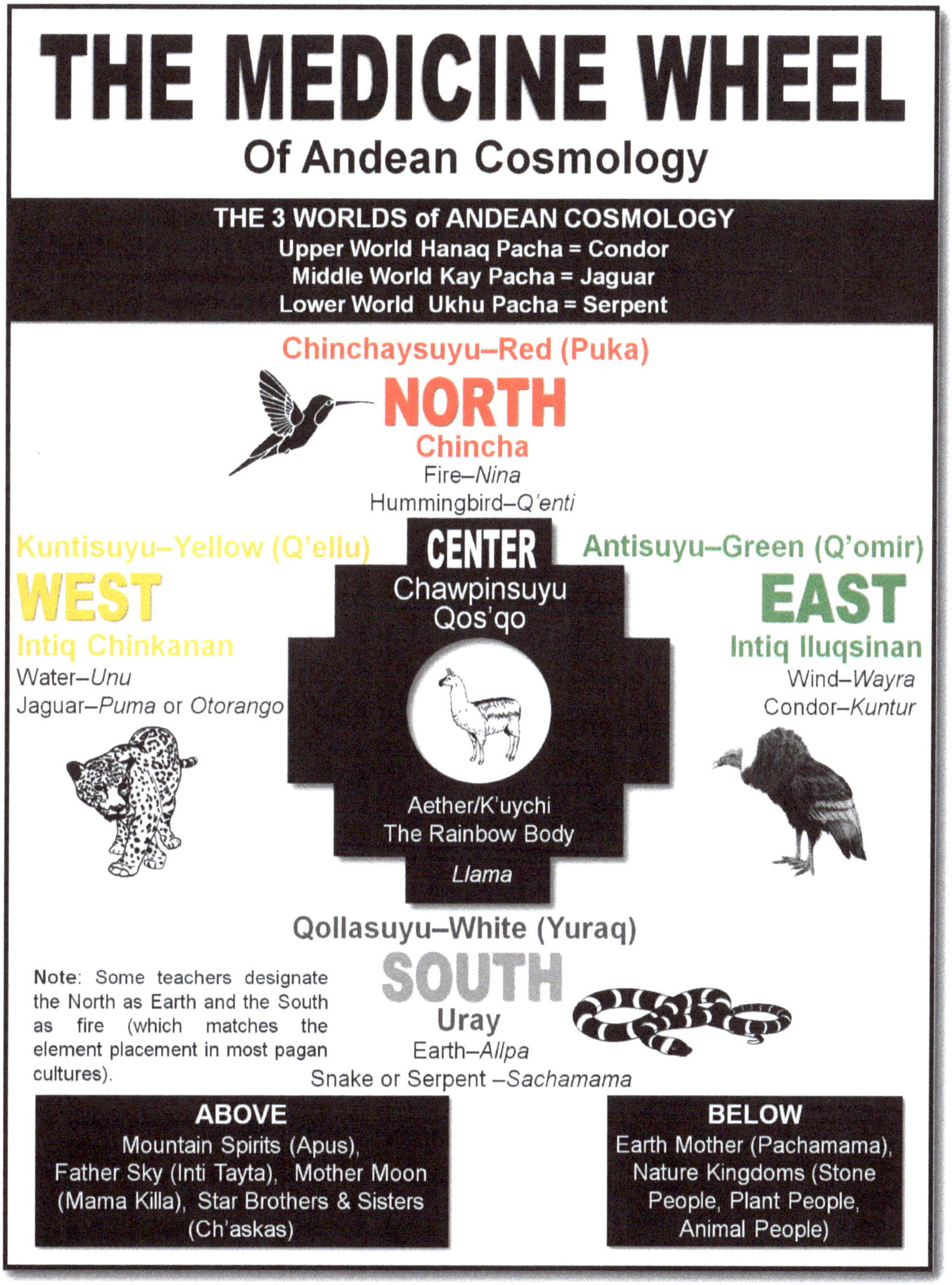

The Andean cosmology recognizes the 3 worlds, with the archetypes of Snake (or Serpent), Jaguar (or Puma), and Condor. The medicine wheel come from North Native American traditions. Anthropologist Alberto Villoldo added a fourth archetype, Hummingbird, to the three archetypes of the Andes to create the four directions for the medicine wheel model. I added the archetype of the Llama to represent the center direction. Llama is a very important support system for the Q'ero and thus represents being in service.

FUN WITH CHUMPIKUNA

Appendixes 115

GLOSSARY

Reference Note: Quechua is the spoken language of indigenous people living in the Andes. It was never a written language therefore many words have multiple spellings. The Quechua terms and their spellings that I have used were verified from the following sources:

- *Quechua Spanish English Dictionary* by Odi Gonzales, Christine Mladie Janney and Emily Fjaellen Thompson
- *Introduction to Quechua: Language of the Andes* by Judith Noble and Jaime Lacasa
- *Quechua Phrasebook* by Lonely Planet
- Online Glossary www.IncaGlossary.org
- Online Dictionary https://en.glosbe.com/en/qu/

Grammatical Note: The plural of original Quechua nouns that end in a consonant is formed by adding "*kuna*". The plural of nouns that end in a vowel is formed in some areas by adding "*kuna*" and in others by the influence of Spanish, by adding "*s*". In this book, I use the plural "*kuna*" for all nouns except *suyu*, which the plural is spelled with the "*s*".

CARDINAL NUMBERS

0	Ch'usaq
1	Huq / Huk / Uh / Uj / Uk
2	Iskay
3	Kinsa / Kimsa
4	Tawa
5	Pisqa / Phisqa / Pichqa
6	Suqta / Soqta / Sohta / Sojta
7	Qanchis
8	Pusaq / Pusaj / Pusah
9	Isqun / Isqon / Isq'on / Hisq'on
10	Chunka
11	Chunka huqniyuq / Chunkauhniyoh
12	Chunka iskayniyuq / Chunkaiskayniyoh

DIRECTIONS

North	Chincha / Chinchay / Wichay
East	Intiq Iluqsinan / Anti
South	Uray / Urin / Qolla
West	Intiq Chinkanan / Kunti / Konti
Center	Chawpi / Chaupi / Chawpinsuyu / Chaupisuyu / Q'osqo / Cusco
Northeast	Antisuyu
Southeast	Qollasuyu / Collasuyu
Southwest	Kuntisuyu / Cuntisuyu / Contisuyu
Northwest	Chinchaysuyu
Behind	Qhepa
Before	Ñawpa
Below	Ura / Hurin
Above	Hawa / Hanan
Left	Lloq'e
Right	Paña
Within	Ukhu
Without	Hawa

DAYS OF THE WEEK

Monday	Killa chaw / Lunisdiya
Tuesday	Ati chaw / Martis
Wednesday	Qoyllur chaw / Mirkulis
Thursday	Illapa chaw / Hwywis
Friday	Ch'aska chaw / Wirnis
Saturday	K'uychi chaw / Sawaru
Sunday	Apu chaw / Inti chaw / Dumingu

MONTHS OF THE YEAR

January	Iniru killa / Qhulla Puquy killa
February	Hiwriru killa / Phiriru killa / Hatun Puquy killa
March	Marsu killa / Pawqar Waray killa
April	Awril killa / Ayriway killa
May	Mayu killa / Aymuray killa
June	Huniyu killa / Inti Raymi killa*
July	Huliyu killa / Anta Situwa killa
August	Awgustu killa / Chakra Yapuy Killa
September	Sitimwri killa / Tarpuy killa
October	Uktuwri killa / Kantaray killa
November	Nuwimbri killa / Ayamarq'a killa
December	Disimwri killa / Qhapaq Raymi killa**

*__Inti Raymi__ Literally, the Festival of the Sun, which is held at the winter solstice in June held at Sacsahuaman, Cusco

**__Qhapaq Raymi (Cápac Raymi)__ A Festival of the Sun, which is held at the summer solstice in December. *Raymi* means a big party. This festivity used to be a celebration of the first month of the Inka calendar.

__Qoyllur Rit'i (Q'ollorit'i)__ Literally, "Snow Star" or "White Star". An annual festival held in the snow at the base of Mount Ausangate to pay tribute to the *apukuna* (mountain spirits) and petition for personal blessings. Tens of thousands of people trek here in late May or early June for the sacred festivities.

SEASONS OF THE YEAR

Spring	Chiraw mit'a / Chiraw pacha
Summer	Ruphay mit'a / Ch'aki pacha
Autumn	Puquy mit'a / Puquy pacha
Winter	Chiri mit'a / Chiri pacha

TIMES OF THE DAY

Sunrise / Dawn	Inti Lloqsimushan / Punchayay / Paqariy / Illariypacha / Inti Siqay / Lluqsiy
Noon	Chawpidiya / Chawpip'unchay / Khuskandiya
Sunset / Nightfall / Dusk	Inti Chinkapushan / Ch'isiyay
Midnight	Khuskantuta / Chawpi Tuta
Day	Diya / P'unchaw / P'unchay
Night	Tuta / Ch'isi

TIME

Past	Ñawpapacha / Qaynapacha
Present	Kunanpacha
Future	Qhipapacha / Hawapacha

COLORS

Black	Yana
Blue	Anqas
Light Blue	Qosi
Brown	Ch'unpi
Gold	Qori / Choqe
Grey or Gray	Oqe / Oqhe / Ch'ihchu
Green	Q'omer
Indigo	Tinaku Ilimphi
Orange	Wallapi
Pink	Puka Llanqa
Purple	Kulli, Sani
Red	Puka
Silver	Qolqe
Transparent	Q'ispi kay
Violet	K'uyu / Kulli
White	Yuraq / Yurah / Yurak or Q'ollo (pure White)
Yellow	Q'ello / Q'ellu / Q'uillu

ELEMENTS

Air, Wind	Wayra / Wyra
Earth	Allpa
Fire	Nina
Spirit	Nuna
Water	Unu, Yaku

DIMENSIONS (SHAMANIC WORLDS)

Upper	Hanaqpacha / Hananpacha (The place of most refined energy)
Middle	Kaypacha (The place where humans live)
Lower	Ukhupacha / Uhupacha (The place of the subconscious and unconscious)

STARS OF THE QOTOKUNA (PLEIADES)

Puriq qoto	Asterope/Sterope 1 and 2 (Sister 1)
Tarpuq qoto	Taygeta (Sister 2)
Ñawi qoto	Maia (Sister 3)
Munay qoto	Celeano (Sister 4)
Llank'aq qoto	Electra (Sister 5)

Yllari qoto	Merope (Sister 6)
K'anchaq qoto	Alcyone (Sister 7)
Mama qoto	Pleione (Mother)
Uraq qoto	Atlas (Father)

LEVELS OF ANDEAN MEDICINE PEOPLE

Paq'o – A first level Andean medicine person who performs energy work on the energy body and soul dis-eases using rituals and medicines from plants and animals

Pampamesayoc – A second level *paq'o*, who specializes in divination and rituals.

Altomesayoc / Altumisayuq – A third level *paq'o*, who has the power to summon the *apukuna* (mountain spirits).

Kurak Akulleq / Kuraz Akulliq – A fourth level *paq'o*, the "great chewer of coca leaves", who is a shapeshifter, having completed their physical manifestations.

Inka Mallku – A fifth level male *paq'o*, who is able to cure by a touch. *Mallku* literally means "tree". There are currently none known to be incarnated at this time. The prophecy is that six of these will be arriving.

Ñust'a – A fifth level female *paq'o*, who is able to cure by a touch. There are currently none known to be incarnated at this time. The prophecy is that six of these will be arriving. *Ñust'a* also refers to Goddesses and female nature spirits.

Sapa Inka – A sixth level male *paq'o*, manifestation of *Inti* (Sun), who brings warmth and light to the world. There are currently none known to be incarnated at this time.

Qoya – A sixth level female *paq'o*, manifestation of *Killa* (Moon) and the Sapa Inka's Queen, who oversees lunar cycles and rituals. There are currently none known to be incarnated at this time.

Taytanchis Ranti – A seventh level *paq'o*, "God of Earth", who is capable of resurrecting their physical bodies after death. There are currently none known to be incarnated at this time.

SAPA INKAS ("The One and Only", Inka term for the King or Emperor. This list excludes those that came after the Spanish Invasion)

1 Manco Cápac (Manqo Qhapaq)	c. 1200–1230
2 Sinchi Roca (Zinchi Roq'a)	c. 1230–1260
3 Lloque Yupanqui (Lloqe Yupanki)	c. 1260–1290
4 Mayta Cápac (Mayta Qhapaq)	c. 1290–1320
5 Cápac Yupanki (Qhapaq Yupanki)	c. 1320–1350
6 Inka Roca (Inka Roq'a)	c. 1350 – c. 1380
7 Yahuár Huacác (Yawar Waqaq)	c. 1380 – c. 1410
8 Wiraqocha Inka (Viracocha Inka)	1410–1438
9 Pachakuti Inka Yupanki (Pachacútec)	1438–1471
10 Tópa Inka (Túpac Yupanqui, Thupa Yupanki)	1471–1493
11 Huayna Cápac (Wayna Qhapaq)	1493–1527

12 Huascár Inka (Waskhar, Wascar, Waskar)   1527–1532
Note: Some consider Atahualpa (Atawallpa), 1532–1533, to be the last Sapa Inka however he came to power by murdering Huascár during the time of the Spanish conquest. He, in turn, was beheaded by the Spaniards. He was followed by six more rulers who were puppets of the Spanish.

MAJOR INKA DEITIES

Ayar Cachi – Hot-tempered God that causes earthquakes
Illapa (Illapu) – Goddess of Lightning and Thunder, God of Weather
Hatun Auki – Great Spirit
Inti (Inti Tayta, Mut'u Inti, Hatun Inti) – Sun God, Father Sun
K'uychi (K'uichi, Cuichu) – Rainbow God
Mama Allpa – Mother Earth, the spirit of the element of earth and soil. *Pachamama* is a cosmological embodiment of the entire Earth system similar to the concept of Gaia.
Mama Killa (Kilya, Quilla) – Mother Moon, Wife of Inti
Mama Kuka – Mother Coca
Mama Ocllo – Wife of Manco Cápac taught women to weave cloth and build houses
Mama Sara – Mother Corn
Mama Tuta – The Dark Void
Manco Cápac – First king of the Inkas taught people how to grow plants, make weapons, work together, and share resources
Pachamama – Earth Mother, the Goddess of Earth and wife of Wiraqocha
Pachatata (Pachacamac, Pachakamak) – Father Sky
Punchao – The God of Day
Qochamama (Mama Qocha) – Sea Mother, Goddess of the Ocean
Sach'amama (Amaru, Mach'aqway) – Mother Tree, Goddess in the shape of a snake with two heads
Wiraqocha (Viracocha) – Literally means "foam of the ocean". Also known as the Supreme Deity, Creator/Creatress, God/Goddess, Kon Tiki, Pachacamac, Tonapa, Taapac, Tupaca, Illa, the Dweller in Space, Lord, Cosmos, the great Source of Everything.
Yakumama (Yacumama) – Water Mother, represented as a snake transformed into a great river when she came to earth. Associated with all of the elements of precipitation in the form of *para* (rain), *rit'i* (snow), or *chikchi* (hail).

GENERAL WORDS

Allpa – Earth.
Ama Suway – Do not steal. One of the three Inka laws.
Ama Qella – Do not be lazy. One of the three Inka laws.
Ama Llulla – Do not lie. One of the three Inka laws.
Api / Hoq'o – Wet. The complementary partner is *Ch'aki*.
Apu – Sacred spirit of the mountain. The plural form is *Apukuna*.

Aura – Latin and Ancient Greek word that literally means "wind, breeze or breath". Energy field that surrounds the physical body. Same as the *poq'po* (energy bubble) in Andean cosmology.

Away – Weaving.

Aya – Cadaver, human remains.

Ayllu – Community, family.

Ayni – Sacred reciprocity or being in right relationship with everyone and everything, similar to the concept of karma.

Ceque / Ceke / Se'qe / Siq'i – Energy lines that radiate out from the center of a sacred site, energy portal, the power of a place or thing.

Cha – Active, ethereal, movement, or energy over time. The complementary partner is *pa*.

Chacra / Chakra – Field or farm, usually with crops growing. (Can be interchangeable with *Pampa*.) Also see *Chakra* below.

Ch'aki – Dry. The complementary partner is *Api*.

Chakana / Chacana – Southern Cross star constellation also call the Stairway.

Chakra – Sanskrit word that literally means "disk", "wheel", or "cycle". Energy centers where the energy body connects to the physical body.

Ch'aska / Q'oyllur – Star. The plural form is *Ch'askakuna*.

Ch'askakancha / Teqsimuyu / Pacha – Universe.

Ch'askakuna / Ch'aska Warani – Stars, constellations, star nations.

Cheqaq / Chiqap – Truth.

Ch'i / Qi – Chinese word for living energy or life force energy.

Chikchi – Hail (noun).

Ch'ily Qocha – Body of water pattern forms a diamond shape in woven textiles.

Chiri / Ch'akiy – Cold. The complementary partner is *Qoñi*.

Ch'ulla – Oneness, a monocot.

Ch'ullu / Ch'ullo – Ceremonial (knit, beaded) hat.

Ch'ullpa / Chulpas / Qollqa – Burial tower or special tomb to bury Inka royalty within. Also a storage container for agricultural products.

Chumpi / Chunpi / Ch'unpi – Belt or brown.

Ch'unchu – Wild, indigenous, jungle dancer, wild indigenous soul. Energy projected outwards.

Conopa / Canopa / Qonopa – Offering.

Collari / Qollari – Wife to the Inka, feminine energy. The complementary partner is *Inkari*.

Hampe / Hampeh / Hampiq – Healer.

Hampi / Jampi – Drug, medicine.

Hanan – Upper part. The complementary partner is *Hurin*.

Hapu – Union of *yanantin* (two dissimilar) energies. The complementary partner is *Ranti*.

Hara / Tanden – Chinese and Japanese character representing the abdomen. It is the energy center in the same area as the *qosqo* (spiritual stomach) in Andean cosmology.

Harchi – Thin. The complementary partner is *pipu*.

Hatun – Big, great, tall.

Hawa – Outside, outer, above, on top of, over, high. The complementary partner is *Ukhu*.

Hiwaya / Jiwaya – Magnetic meteorite stone.

Huaca / Wak'a – Localized or held energy, the power of a place or thing, much like a sacred site or an energy portal.

Huamanga – An alabaster limestone from which many Andean carvings are made.

Hucha – Dense, heavy, or incompatible energy; energy that does not serve. *Hucha* is a product of negative or lower energy emotions. Literally, failure to follow through, sin. The complimentary partner is *sami*.

Hucha Mikhuy or Mihuy – The process of "digesting" energy using one's *qosqo* (spiritual stomach) and separating energy into two streams: One, the *sami* (high vibratory energy) ascends and two, the *hucha* (heavy dense energy) descends. This is a process that the *paq'okuna* (Andean medicine people) learn to bring energy back into *ayni* (right relationship).

Hurin – Lower part. The complimentary partner is *Hanan*.

Ida – One of the three most important *nadis* (energy channels) of the energy body in Hindu cosmology. *Ida* represents the lunar, feminine, and right brain.

Illapa – Lightning.

Inka – King, son of the Sun, the soul. The complimentary partner is *Qoya*.

Inkari – The Inka, masculine energy. The complimentary partner is *Collari*.

Inti – Sun.

Inti Chinkapushan – Dusk, shadow, and light falling or receding from the viewer.

Inti Lloqsimushan – Dawn, sunlight, and light lifting or advancing toward the viewer.

Itu – A masculine nature spirit. The complementary partner is *pacarino*.

Kallari – Flow, change, movement.

K'anchay – Light energy analogous to celestial energy. Literally, to shine.

Karpay / Qarpay – An energetic transmission or rite through the ancient Inka lineage. Literally means irrigation or watering. The purpose of transmitting living energy is to irrigate an individual's Inka seed so it can sprout.

Kawak / Qhawaq – Seer, clairvoyant, visionary.

Kawsay – Living energy, vital life force, life, exist.

Kawsaypacha – The sea of living energy or life force that surrounds and permeates all things. It animates or moves time and space, and it is what makes everything happen. Also, the term for ceremonial dress and ornamentation because it is how one presents oneself in the world.

Khuya – A stone that is used for healing and/or communicating an intention. These sacred objects are considered to be fully conscious, and able to communicate and teach.

Ki – Japanese word for living energy or life force energy.

Killa / Quilla – Moon or month.

Killapura – Full moon. The complimentary partner is *Killawañuy*.

Killawañuy – New moon. The complimentary partner is *Killapura*.

K'intu – Coca leaves used for prayers and ceremony.

Kimsañeqe Ñawi / Kimsa Kah Ñawi / Iskay Qhepa Ñawi – Third Eye.

K'uchu – Point or corner.

Kuka – Coca.

Kundalini – Sanskrit word that literally means "coiled snake". Divine feminine energy coiled up at the base of the spine.

Kunka – Throat

Kuntur – Condor. Also called *Hatun* (Great) *Kuntur*.

Kurak / Kuraq – An elder.

Kutiy / Kuti – Time; returning or coming back.

K'uychi / K'uichi – Rainbow.

Lirpuy – Reflect. Complimentary partner is *Ukyay*.

Llama – A member of the camelid family, which also includes alpaca and vicuña.

Llank'ay, Llankay, Llancay, Llancai, Llamk'ay, Llamkay – Way in the world, body, *hara,* right action.

Llank'i – Smooth. The complimentary partner is *Qhasqa*.

Llaqta – Village, city, town, birthplace.

Machuyasqa – Male elder. The complimentary partner is *Payayasqa*.

Maki – Hand. *Makikuna* is hands (plural).

Masintin – A joining together of similar energies or entities into a harmonious relationship. The complimentary partner is *yanantin*.

Maqana Rumi – Fighting stone used in the *warak'a* (braided sling).

Merkaba – Composed of three separate words: *Mer*, which means "light"; *Ka*, which means "spirit" and *Ba*, which means "body". From Jewish mysticism, the merkaba literally means "chariot". It is a 6-pointed star vehicle of light that provides transport for the energy body in other dimensions.

Mesa / Misha / Misa Qepe / Misa Qipi – Sacred bundle that opens into an altar. *Note:* "*mesa*" is the Spanish term.

Mesayoc / Mesayoq – A *paq'o's* (Andean medicine person's) quest for power through the *mesa* (Andean medicine bundle).

Mink'a – In need, ability to receive, system of mutual help.

Mit'a – Shift of work, public labor. Service to *ayllu* (community) and the world. Also, seasons or time period.

Mosoq Karpay – Literally means "new initiation", a rite of passage to raise consciousness to the fifth level. Also, the time when the *Inka Mallku* and *Nust'a* will arrive.

Mu – Coming toward. Literally, in this direction. The complimentary partner is *pu*.

Muju / Ruru – Seed.

Mullu – Spondylus (spiny oyster) shell.

Munay – Love, spirit, heart, heart-alignment, right intention.

Munay Ki – *Munay* means "heart" and *Ki* means "energy" or "motion". Together they become the energy of unconditional love in motion. A system of energetic transmissions taught by The Four Winds school.

Muyuma – Spiral.

Nadi – Sanskrit word that literally means "stream". There are fourteen principal energy pathways, of which *ida*, *pingala* and *sushumna* are considered the most important.

Ñawi – Eye, energy center (analogous to energy *chakras*). The plural form is *Ñawikuna*.

Nunapukacha – Spiritual world.

Otorongo / Uturunku / Uturunqu Chinchay – Jaguar. *Choquechinchay, chocachinchay,* or *chuquichinchay* is the golden jaguar. **Note**: There are several different breeds of big cats found in the Americas. The jaguar is part of the *panthera* family, which is only found in Central and South America. It is golden-coated with spots. It looks very similar to a leopard, that is found in Africa and Asia, but has a rounder face. Also found in the *panthera* family is the panther, which is a black-coated jaguar. The Andean people usually call the big cat that is engraved on objects as the "puma". However, it usually has spots carved on it as well, and that would indicate that they are really referring to a jaguar. In the case of the *chumpi* stones, the name of image can be used interchangeable depending on your personal preference.

Pa – Calm, ground, potential or space. The complementary partner is *Cha*.

Pacarina / Pakarina – A feminine nature spirit. The complementary partner is *Itu*.

Pacha – Two worlds coming together to create a whole; a dimension of Space and Time. *Pacha* can mean world, age, Cosmos, earth, nature, space, universe, era, place, or time.

Pachakuti / Pachacuti / Pachakutiy – An overturning of space-time or a period of cosmic transformation that affects Earth and human consciousness. Also, the name of the ninth Inka emperor, Transformer of the World.

Pallay – Woven patterns, structure. Literally, to pick, harvest. The complementary partner is *pampa*.

Pallay Tukuy – Finishing design in woven textiles.

Pampa / Panpa – Flat field, plain. (Can be interchangeable with *chacra*.) The complementary partner is *Pallay*.

Paq'o – Shaman, mystic, Andean priest, or medicine person.

Para – Rain.

Psychopomp – Greek word meaning "guide of souls". The main role of a psychopomp is to assist other souls passing out of this physical world and moving into the spiritual world.

Payayasqa – Female elder. The complementary partner is *Machuyasqa*.

Phaqcha / Paqcha – Waterfall.

Phukuy – Prayerful breath created by blowing from the mouth usually with a spiritual essence such as Florida water.

Phutuy – Germination.

Pichay – To clean, sweep, or erase.

Pingala – One of the three most important *nadis* (energy channels) of the energy body in Hindu cosmology. *Pingala* represents the solar, masculine, and left brain,

Pipu / Rakhu —Thick. The complimentary partner is *Harchi*.

Poq'po – The bubble of energy surrounding and infusing the physical body. The energy body or luminous energy field.

Prana – Hindu word for living energy or life force energy.

Pu – Moving away. Literally, it, them. The complimentary partner is *Mu*.

Puma – Cougar or Mountain Lion. This cat belongs in the *Puma concolor* family and is found in both North and South America. It has a plain tan or brown coat of fur. Please see note about big cats under *Otorongo*.

Punchay – Day, light. The complementary partner is *Tuta*.

Q'enti / Q'ente – Hummingbird. Also called *Siwar* (Royal) *Q'enti*.

Q'ero – Indigenous people of the Andes who originate from the spiritual advisors to the Inka.

Qhapaq Ñan – Inka Road, rich pathway, valuable way.

Qhari – Man, husband, masculine. The complimentary partner is *Warmi*.

Qhasqa / Q'asqa – Rough. The complimentary partner is *Llank'i*.

Qhuyay – To love or deeply care for.

Q'illay – Metal.

Qiqlla – Mineral.

Qiru / K'ullu / L'lanta – Wood.

Qocha / Cocha – Body of water, lake, lagoon. Energy collected and held. Creates a diamond pattern in woven textiles.

Qoñi – Warm. The complimentary partner is *Chiri*.

Qora – Plant (noun).

Qosqo / Cusco / Cuzco – Center of the Inka Empire, the navel of the world, our spiritual stomach.

Qoya – Queen, sister/wife of the Inka. The complimentary partner is *Inka*.

Quechua / Quichua – A language of the Andean indigenous people. It is also called *Runasimi*, literally the "language of the people", by the indigenous peoples.

Ranti – Union of *masintin* (two similar) energies. The complementary partner is *Hapu*.

Rit'i – Snow.

Rumi – Stone.

Runa – Human. The plural form is *Runakuna*, i.e. people.

Saiwa / Saywa – Column of energy, usually connects the three shamanic worlds and bridges the physical to the spiritual worlds.

Saiwachakuy – Creating a column of energy that ascends from *Pachamama* (Mother Earth), through the *poq'po* (energy body) to the Cosmos. The complimentary partner is *Saminchakuy*.

Saminchakuy – Creating a column of energy descending from the Cosmos to the *poq'po*. This displaces *hucha* (dense energy) in the *poq'po* to *Pachamama* (Mother Earth), who can transmute it. The complimentary partner is *Saiwachakuy*.

Sami – Fine, high vibratory energy; subtle spiritual energy; energy that serves one's destiny. Literally, good fortune, happiness. The complimentary partner is *Hucha*.

Sara – Corn, maize.

Sayaqruna – Adulthood.

Shushuma – One of the three most important *nadis* (energy channels) of the energy body in Hindu cosmology. *Shushuma* is the central channel through which kundalini energy can run through.

Siki – Tailbone, buttocks.

Suyu / Suyo – Region, division, territory of the Inka Empire. See also *Tawantinsuyu*.

Taraña – Saddle of *warak'a* (braided sling).

Taripaypacha – The place where we "Meet Ourselves Again." The great new age of awareness following the *Pachakuti* or the turning over of time and space.

Tawantin – Four. The harmonious union of four energies.

Tawantinsuyu – The four regions of the Inka Empire. Consists of the *Antisuyu* (Northeast), *Qollasuyu* or *Collasuyu* (Southeast), *Kuntisuyu* or *Cuntisuyu* (Southwest), *Chinchaysuyu* (Northwest), with *Qosqo* (Cusco) as the *Chawpinsuyu* (center).

Tawa Inti Qocha – Four sun lake, a woven textile pattern.

Taway – Dice.

Teqse – Global.

Tiha – Tile.

T'ika – Flower or tassels on textiles.

Tupanaqui – To tap.

Tuta – Night, dark. The complementary partner is *Punchay*.

Ukhu – Inside, inner, interior, deep. The complementary partner is *Hawa*.

Ukyay – Absorb. (Note: The only source I found citing the Quechua term for "absorb" said that "*ukyay*" is a tentative translation.) Complimentary partner is *Lirpuy*.

Ura – Below.

Uywa – Animal.

Wachakuy / Paqariy – Birth. The complementary partner is *Wañuy*.

Wañuy – Death. The complimentary partner is *Wachakuy*.

Warak'a / Warakha – Braided sling. The Spanish term is *Boleadora*.

Warma – Adolescence.

Warmi – Woman, wife, feminine. The complimentary partner is *Qhari*.

Wasi – House.

Waska / Waskha – Rope

Wawa / Ch'ete / Ch'iti – Child.

Willka – Sacred.

Wiñay – Grow, develop.

Yachay – Vision, wisdom, mind, head, right thought.

Yanantin – A joining together of opposite or dissimilar energies or entities into a harmonious relationship. The complimentary partner is *Masintin*.

Yang – Chinese word for masculine principles of the Universe.

Yin – Chinese word for feminine principles of the Universe.

Yoc / Yoq – Power possessed by or flowing through, usually relating to shamanic power.

–yoc / –yoq – Used as a suffix means having the property of or possessing.

Yumay – Conception.

Yupay – Numbers.

REFERENCE LINKS

YOUTUBE VIDEOS ON CHUMPI STONES

Listen to Robert Wakeley Wheeler talk about *chumpi* stones
https://www.youtube.com/watch?v=JdETYZxWxQk

Watch Don Andres Espinoza perform a *chumpi away* ritual on Juan Núñez del Prado
https://www.youtube.com/watch?v=0n2id2H52f0

Watch Jorge Luis Delgado perform a *chumpi* away ritual
https://www.youtube.com/watch?v=Vft0WHDJh-8

WHERE TO PURCHASE CHUMPI STONE SETS

 **Sacred Pathways:** www.SacredPathways.us/shop/

 **The Shaman's Market:** www.ShamansMarket.com

 **Shaman Dealer:** www.ShamanDealer.com

 **eBay:** www.eBay.com

 **Amazon:** www.Amazon.com

 **Etsy:** www.Etsy.com

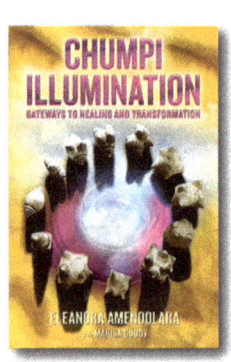

Sacred Center: https://sacredcenter.net

Eleanora Amendolara is author of *Chumpi Illumination Gateways to Healing and Transformation* Book and Wisdom Card Deck

WISDOM WEAVER PRESS OFFERINGS

THE CHUMPI STONE GUIDEBOOK: Carved Companions from the Andes

The Chumpi Stone Guidebook is a reference guide about Andean sacred carved items and their imagery. It is an exploration of how to integrate these fascinating stones into your 21st century lifestyle. It includes:

- Description, interpretation, and correspondences for *Chumpi* Stones.
- Uses, both ancient and modern, for *Chumpi* Stones.
- Fully illustrated directory of imagery carved on stones, dice, and other items from Andean culture.
- A comparison of the human energy systems from Andean and Hindu cosmology that influence Western beliefs.

This book is available in both the printed version (p-book) and the electronic version (e-book).

Website: www.ChumpiSacredStones.com

Available at: www.Amazon.com, www.BarnesandNoble.com, and Apple iTunes.

SOUL SEX: The Alchemy of Gender & Sexuality

A Guidebook for Identity Fluidity in the 21st Century

Soul Sex offers fresh perspectives on gender and sexual identity, including biological, sociological, and psychological influences with an emphasis on spiritual impacts. Included are new concepts about gender fluidity and alternative sexual orientations. The author draws on years of research and personal experience to create the broadest perspective of gender and sexual identity compiled in one volume.

This book is available in both the printed version (p-book) and the electronic version (e-book).

Website: www.SoulSexAlchemy.com

Available at: www.Amazon.com, www.BarnesandNoble.com, and Apple iTunes.

THE CHAKANA ORACLE GUIDEBOOK: Ancient Wisdom for the 21st Century

The Chakana Oracle Guidebook is a reference guide rich with new perspectives on the Andean cosmology and the indigenous Andean Lineage, whose roots go back over 500 years to the Inka Empire. It also serves as a companion to *The Chakana Oracle Card Deck*. It includes:

- In-depth information with full-color illustrations of Andean cosmology and symbology.
- Layouts for divination work with a foundation that is based on the geography of the terrestrial overlaid with the energy of the celestial.
- Description, interpretation, and practice for each of the 100 oracle cards.

This guidebook is available in both the printed version (p-book) and the electronic version (e-book).

Website: www.ChakanaOracle.com

Available at: www.SacredPathways.us/shop, www.Amazon.com, www.BarnesandNoble.com, and Apple iTunes.

THE CHAKANA ORACLE 101 CARD DECK: Ancient Wisdom for the 21st Century

The Chakana Oracle is designed to create a connection from the user to the voices of the indigenous Andean Lineage, whose roots go back over 500 years to the Inka Empire. Each card includes a photograph of an energetic companion from the Andean cultural tradition as well as its name in the native language of Quechua and in English. Energetic companions are aids that help the user activate, animate, and move energy within different grids of time, dimensions, and portals. These cards are printed on linen card stock to imitate the texture of woven cloth that is so vital to the Andean culture.

Website: www.ChakanaOracle.com

Available at: www.SacredPathways.us/shop

ACKNOWLEDGEMENTS

I could not have completed this book without the support and guidance of many individuals to whom I would like to express my deepest gratitude:

Robert Wakeley Wheeler (Wake) – Wake is the co-author of our book and card deck entitled *The Chakana Oracle*. As a result of his 20-plus years of experience traveling and working with the indigenous people in the Andes, he has become one of the foremost teachers of Andean cosmology from a Western viewpoint. He has been a mentor to me, greatly expanding my interest and knowledge of Andean cosmology. Wake is a subject matter expert on the *mesa* (sacred bundle) and Andean textiles. He is a steward of the Andean spiritual customs, practicing them every single day. Wake's website is www.SacredPathways.us.

The Q'ero and their Lineage – The spokespeople for the Q'ero nation who have supported my journey are don Francisco Chura Flores, doña Juanita Apaza Ccapa, don Eduardo Chura Apaza, and Wilbert Salas Atasi (author of *The Andean Tradition in the New World*). Their guidance and friendship have been a momentous inspiration for my work.

The carving artisans – Much appreciation and gratitude go to the indigenous carvers of the Andes, many of them unknown, that produce *chumpi* stones, *taway* (dice), *conopakuna* (votive offerings), *tiha rumi* (tile stones) and other sacred items.

The weavers of energy – Much appreciation and gratitude go to the indigenous weavers in the Andes, who have produced beautiful textiles for over 500 years. Nilda Callañaupa Alvarez is the director of the *Centro de Textiles Tradicionales del Cusco* (CTTC), which she established to preserve the ancient textile arts. She represents ten weaving villages in the Andes. Her vast knowledge is invaluable to understanding the art of textile creation in the Andes. The webpage for the CTTC is www.TextilesCusco.org. Nilda has written many books, including *Faces of Tradition: Weaving Elders of the Andes, Secrets of Spinning, Weaving, and Knitting in the Peruvian Highlands, Textile Traditions of Chinchero: A Living Heritage, Weaving in the Peruvian Highlands: Dreaming Patterns, Weaving Memories,* and *Weaving Lives: Traditional Textiles of Cusco.*

Beta Readers – The beta readers for this project were Krista Nielsen, Jim Hagedorn and Carol Brzezinski (www.FireCircleMedia.com), and Mariela Maya (author of *Practical Guide to the Tzolkin,* www.MayanKin.com). I thank them for their knowledge and time in reviewing this book. Their feedback had a huge impact on the final presentation of the material.

Lastly, I would like to acknowledge and thank my Indigenous Soul, my personal Ancestor Lineage, and my Guiding Spirits. Their support for my spiritual journey on Earth always provides me with strength, guidance, wisdom, and inspiration.

ABOUT THE AUTHOR

Web: www.DrakeInnerprizes.com
Email: DrakeBearStephen@pacbell.net

Drake is a Transpersonal Hypnotherapist, Shamanic Energy Medicine Practitioner, NLP practitioner, and a Reiki Master. Drake has a variety of background experiences that includes a 37-year career in telecommunications and a B.A. from Antioch University in art and psychology. Drake's introduction to shamanism began over 18 years ago with an interest in Two Spirits because they identifies as pan-gendered. Their preferred pronouns are the singular they, their, and them.

Drake specializes in past life therapy and has a private practice that focuses on energy medicine and self-empowerment. Drake also teaches workshops on gender and sexual identity, the Afterlife, and other topics of transpersonal metaphysics. Drake is the author of *Soul Sex: The Alchemy of Gender and Sexuality* and co-author of *The Chakana Oracle Guidebook and Card Deck*. In addition, Drake is a contributor to *TRANScestors: Navigating LGBTQ+ Aging, Illness, and End of Life Decisions Volume 2*. Drake is also a photographer, illustrator, and artist that produces their own websites and advertising materials. Drake is at work on two new books, *The Gender Oracle Guidebook and Card Deck* and *Wisdom to Die For,* a modern book of the dead.

TUPANANCHIS-KAMA

(Until We Meet Again)

www.ingramcontent.com/pod-product-compliance
Lightning Source LLC
Chambersburg PA
CBHW061812290426
44110CB00026B/2858